THE SOUTHEAST
Native Plant Primer

THE SOUTHEAST
Native Plant Primer

225 Plants for an Earth-Friendly Garden

LARRY MELLICHAMP AND PAULA GROSS
PHOTOGRAPHS BY WILL STUART

Timber Press
Portland, Oregon

Frontispiece: Native perennials make for a sea of color in Southeast gardens.

Opposite: Red-yellow blooms of cross-vine (*Bignonia capreolata*) intertwine with American wisteria (*Wisteria frutescens*) in a colorful display.

Page 6 (clockwise from top left): An eastern tiger swallowtail is attracted to a cutleaf coneflower (*Rudbeckia lacinata*); cheery bloodroot (*Sanguinaria canadensis*) is a popular harbinger of spring; silverleaf mountain mint (*Pycnanthemum incanum*) is a favorite of the common eastern bumblebee; Florida anisetree (*Illicium floridanum*) is known for its strongly scented leaves.

Timber Press
Workman Publishing
Hachette Book Group, Inc.
1290 Avenue of the Americas
New York, New York 10104
timberpress.com

Printed in China on responsibly sourced paper
Third printing 2024
Cover design by Amy Sly
Text design by Debbie Berne

The Hachette Speakers Bureau provides a wide range of authors for speaking events. To find out more, go to hachettespeakersbureau.com or email hachettespeakers@hbgusa.com.

ISBN 978-1-60469-991-3

Catalog records for this book are available from the Library of Congress.

For Suzanne, Harrison, William, and Elizabeth.
And to all the children of Mother Earth.
May you cherish her and strengthen
the threads that connect us all.

Contents

Introduction

This book is about native plants in the Southeast and how to select and use them in the home landscape. While we could easily get lost in reverie for the abundance and beauty of this flora, with its magnolias, hydrangeas, and coneflowers, it's important that we focus on you. Whether you've just bought your first trowel or are on your third pair of pruners, you are a gardener. This book is a tool—part garden coach, part hand-picked plant palette, and part visual inspiration. It's a starting point or perhaps a new path in your partnership with plants. We hope it will ignite your curiosity to dig in the dirt and to dig deeper into what interests you. There are field guides and trails, Master Gardener classes, native plant societies and gardens, and new friendships to explore.

You never know what plant may inspire you, native or non-native. We offer you these southeastern plant species that inspire us. Many native plants have become mainstays of the gardening world and interest in those that haven't yet is on the rise. Their beauty is apparent, yet we look to natives because we know our landscapes can and should do so much more than please our senses. Our gardens are part of the web of life and can provide food, shelter, and nurseries for pollinators, birds, and other creatures, and they can do this without demanding excessive inputs. We can choose plants that are good neighbors, that don't readily escape our gardens and degrade other habitats. Growing such a garden is a deeply satisfying experience when you embrace connection over perfection. The truth is, you are a part of the web of life, too. Welcome your family and friends into the garden as a place to feel at home among the abundance of native plants.

◄ Spring ephemerals native to the Southeast are a welcome sight in woodland gardens.

What Is a Native Plant?

Whether the draw of native plants has been lifelong or is a brand-new fascination, the question of just what a native plant is will come up. Our definition is simple: a species is native to the Southeast if it was growing in the region before European settlement. The plant might have come by physical forces of nature or by the activities of animals and indigenous humans, but it lives and reproduces on its own and seems to fit in with the other native flora and fauna. Plants that evolved in Asia, Africa, Europe, and South America are non-natives, or what we call exotics. Sometimes exotic plants establish themselves locally and reproduce in the wild. We refer to those as naturalized, but that doesn't make them native. For example, both oxeye daisy and Queen Anne's lace are thoroughly naturalized in the Southeast (and sometimes called wildflowers), but we know that they are natives of Europe, not North America. Unfortunately, some exotic plants go much further than just establishing themselves and reproducing in the wild—they take over. We're talking about invasive exotic plants, invasives for short. Think kudzu, Japanese honeysuckle, and Chinese privet. By reproducing prolifically, sucking up resources, and growing unchecked due to a lack of their native predators, invasive plants crowd out native plants. This results in displacing those native insects, birds, and other animals that depend on natives. The end result is often a degraded habitat unable to support much biological diversity. When mixing native and non-native plants in your garden (as we do), be certain you don't include invasive species. Even if you think you can control them, the risk is too high. You may not even realize they have escaped by sending seeds flowing down the creek or being carried off by birds, for example.

The region covered in this book is at once traditional, and then again arbitrary. The Southeast certainly includes Virginia, North Carolina, Tennessee, South Carolina,

◄ A meadow filled with southeastern native plants welcomes visitors in late summer.

Georgia, Alabama, northern Florida, and Mississippi. This is arbitrary, in that plants don't understand state boundaries! In fact, a great many of the species native to the Southeast are also native to the Northeast and Midwest. We've chosen to include a few species that are native just outside our defined boundaries, like threadleaf bluestar and giant coneflower from the southern Midwest, because they are outstanding, well-behaved garden plants in the Southeast.

The more you learn about the natural history of plants, the more you'll find that change is at the heart of it. Drawing hard boundary lines is impractical—these plants are moving targets. Wind and migrating birds continually carry seeds about, and occasional plant establishments occur in what seem to be isolated regions. For example, the scarlet hibiscus grows among other natives in south-central North Carolina, far from its primary Gulf Coast range. How the hibiscus got that far inland is a mystery. Does this species count as native? We think it has to. It may seem oddly out of place, and we don't know when and how it got here, but it is reasonable for it to be here. We use the maps at the Biota of North America, bonap.org, to check the latest distributions of plants. For a simple check on where a plant is recorded native, we also recommend wildflower.org, or the USDA PLANTS database.

It doesn't matter much to us whether a plant can be proven a longtime native to a narrow region, as long as it came from somewhere reasonably close and fits in with the flora without being an obnoxious weed. By now, humans have disturbed so much native habitat and spread so many plants around in various activities including gardening, agriculture, military maneuvers, and simple family vacations, that it wouldn't be surprising to find almost anything almost anywhere in any almost-suitable habitat. However, it's this very disturbance of native habitat and its impact on biodiversity that calls us to consider more thoughtfully what we grow in our own backyards. Those backyards cannot replace large tracts of native habitat, but they *can* support a greater diversity of living organisms than most currently do, and native plants have a foundational role to play.

Why grow natives?

There are many compelling reasons for choosing natives, but at the end of the day we grow them because they are simply beautiful plants with attractive flowers, foliage, and fruit—local plants with seasonal appeal, much like locally grown foods. There's enough variety to fill every niche in a garden, and chances are you are already growing some. If you've got black-eyed Susan, summer phlox, or dogwood, you're growing natives.

Peel back this layer of natural beauty, and you'll discover several more reasons for choosing native plants. There's no question that native insects rely much more on native plants than on exotics. The larvae of many butterflies and moths, for example, will eat only native species. And all baby birds depend on a steady diet of insect larvae to reach adulthood. There has been a decline in certain native insects because their habitats and food plants have been lost to development. This drop in pollinator species and numbers, both native and exotic, is especially alarming considering the vital role they play in our food production. According to the Food and Agriculture Organization of the United Nations (FAO), 35 percent of global food production depends on pollinators, and between 15 and 40 percent of insect pollinator species are threatened with extinction.

Dr. Douglas Tallamy's book *Bringing Nature Home* is a startling revelation of the damage that overuse of exotics and sterile expanses of lawns in the home landscape have done to natural plant-animal associations. When it was published, his book created something of a mini-firestorm, stimulating deep commitment in many people to do something about the overplanting of exotics and to try to reverse the decline in the diversity of native birds and insects. These creatures are intricately linked in the web of life, as are we all, and disruption in those interactions can weaken the whole system.

The remedy, according to Tallamy, is to plant more natives, create islands of diverse vegetation in a sea of urban uniformity, and let native birds and insects eat a little bit of our property. We have absolutely no problem with that. In fact, it's empowering to know we can actually do something to support these creatures, right here, right now.

As part of this web, we are responsible for what we're putting in and taking out of our lands—excessive water, gas to power engines, and chemicals like fertilizers, pesticides, and herbicides. If one of your goals is to minimize these inputs, choosing the correct native plants can support that. You may have heard that native plants are tough—that they don't need the water, fertilizer, pest control, or pampering of other plants. Like any generalization, there is some truth and some half-truth in that statement. Plants are adapted to particular niches—some broad, some narrow. In any habitat, you'll find both abundant and rare species. In other words, natives run the gamut from highly adaptive in a variety of conditions to practically ungrowable outside the wild. It's true that natives don't require our inputs or maintenance when growing in their natural habitats. But once we bring them into our highly disturbed habitats, with our aesthetic standards, they are garden plants and require a basic amount of maintenance to grow and perform to our desires. One benefit they do offer over exotics is in weathering climate extremes like droughts and cold snaps. In the Southeast, warm winter spells followed by late freezes regularly damage flower buds of exotics like saucer magnolias and new growth of crepe myrtles. Native species aren't fooled by those temperature swings and emerge unscathed. A well-sited native plant in a landscape has staying power, which saves money and effort over the long run.

Lowering your inputs and maintenance is really about choosing the right plant for the right place and making sure it gets good care in its first year. After that, appropriately sited native plants rarely require supplemental water, and a once-a-year top-dressing with compost is fertilizer enough. By choosing natives, you can be certain you are not contributing to the spread of invasive species and the havoc they can wreak in vulnerable habitats. Growing a variety of plants, as opposed to the top ten exotic usual suspects, will support a diversity of insects. This often keeps a fair

It's easier for a hungry prothonotary warbler to find food in a garden of native plants.

Native plants flourish in a naturalistic garden and help create a sense of abundance.

balance between pests and beneficial insects so you don't need to intervene, especially not with insecticides that kill the good bugs along with the pests. A few caterpillar holes and aphid congregations are reminders that birds are being fed, and you're likely to see ladybugs flying about.

Finally, native plants provide a sense of place that can be reassuring in our age of rapid and frequent mobility. When you're in your garden, sharing space with plants that have been in the Southeast for many thousands of years,

you're a part of that history. We love being reminded of the natural habitats of the plants, birds, mammals, and insects in our gardens. Native plants are part of a community, all interacting. Never forget that a species in cultivation has a home somewhere in the wild, where it is adapted to a particular set of environmental conditions. The only reason we can grow it in our gardens is that it is adaptable enough to accommodate the less-than-perfect conditions we provide. And for this ability we are eternally grateful.

Invasive Species and Native Alternatives

Chances are you have at least one invasive plant species growing on your property. To learn more about which plants are serious problems in your part of the Southeast, visit www.se-eppc.org. If you've got them in your garden, chip away at eradicating them so they won't have a chance to spread into adjacent habitats. Many of our worst invasive species would never be sold in nurseries today (it's hard to find kudzu for sale), but unfortunately some serious invaders still are. The following chart gives you some native alternatives to invasive species (depending on your location) that you might run across at the garden center.

INVASIVE SPECIES	NATIVE ALTERNATIVES
autumn olive (*Elaeagnus umbellata*), thorny olive (*Elaeagnus pungens*)	yaupon holly (*Ilex vomitoria*), arrowwood (*Viburnum dentatum*), Florida anise (*Illicium floridanum*)
'Bradford' pear (*Pyrus calleryana* 'Bradford') and related cultivars	dogwood (*Cornus florida*), two-winged silverbell (*Halesia diptera*), redbuds (*Cercis canadensis*)
Chinese wisteria (*Wisteria sinensis*)	American wisteria (*Wisteria frutescens*)
eulalia grass (*Miscanthus sinensis*)	switch grass (*Panicum virgatum*), muhly grass (*Muhlenbergia capillaris*), little bluestem (*Schizachyrium scoparium*)
Japanese blood grass (*Imperata cylindrica* 'Rubra')	red switch grass (*Panicum* 'Shenandoah', *P.* 'Cheyenne Sky')
Japanese honeysuckle (*Lonicera japonica*)	For climbing and color: coral honeysuckle (*Lonicera sempervirens*), yellow jessamine (*Gelsemium sempervirens*). For fragrance: coastal sweet-pepperbush (*Clethra alnifolia*).
mimosa (*Albizia julibrissin*)	redbud (*Cercis canadensis*), fringe tree (*Chionanthus virginicus*)
nandina (*Nandina domestica*)	dwarf yaupon holly (*Ilex vomitoria* 'Nana') oakleaf hydrangea (*Hydrangea quercifolia*), beautyberry (*Callicarpa americana*)
privet (*Ligustrum sinense*, *L. japonicum*)	yaupon holly (*Ilex vomitoria*), common wax-myrtle (*Morella cerifera*), Walter's viburnum (*Viburnum obovatum*), Carolina cherry-laurel (*Prunus caroliniana*)
Vines: chocolate vine (*Akebia quinata*), oriental bittersweet (*Celastrus orbiculatus*), Japanese climbing fern (*Lygodium japonicum*), variegated porcelain berry (*Ampelopsis brevipedunculata* 'Elegans'), English ivy (*Hedera helix*)	cross-vine (*Bignonia capreolata*), yellow jessamine (*Gelsemium sempervirens*), climbing hydrangea (*Decumaria barbara*), muscadine grape (*Muscadinia rotundifolia*)

Red switch grass 'Shenandoah' offers beautiful color and texture in conditions from dry soils and full sun to rain gardens.

Regions and habitats of the Southeast

The Southeast is a diverse region for plant habitats. It can be divided into regions based on topography, soil, and bedrock type. These are the regions that we use when giving the natural ranges of species. Which do you currently call home?

The **Coastal Plain** is fairly uniform in its flatness, with well-drained, sandy-loam soils stretching along the coastline and up the Mississippi corridor. The Sandhills region within the Coastal Plain is a narrow belt just inland, where deep white sand accumulated along an ancient shoreline.

The **Piedmont**, literally "foot of the mountains," is a wide region of rolling hills and small leftover remnants of worn-down mountains. The soils are more clay based.

The **Southern Appalachian Mountains** are ancient formations of mostly granite-based rocks, eroded and rounded over 250 million years. They have never been glaciated or flooded. Changes in elevation and north-to-south slope exposures provide many diverse habitats for plants in a cool, moist climate.

Ridge, valley, and plateau regions in Tennessee and Northern Alabama are underlain by limestone rocks and provide diverse habitats much like the Piedmont, but with rich soils of a less acidic nature.

Within these physical regions are recognizable habitats. Using the broadest strokes, we simply refer to them as fields, forests, swamps, and marshes. For the purpose of informing our choices of garden plants, this is usually specific enough. If you'd like to learn more about habitats within the mountains, the Piedmont, and the Coastal Plain, and the plants that grow there, we recommend the introduction section of any of the following plant guides: *Wildflowers of the Atlantic Southeast,* by Cotterman, Waitt, and Weakley; *Wildflowers and Plant Communities of the Southern Appalachian Mountains and Piedmont*, by Timothy Spira; *A Guide to the Wildflowers of South Carolina*, by Richard Porcher and Douglas Rayner; or *Southeastern Wildflowers*, by Jan Midgely.

Knowing which region you call home and the habitat of the plant you're hoping to grow are useful bits of intersecting information. If you're having difficulty growing a mountain species in the Coastal Plain, there's a good reason and it doesn't have to do with the color of your thumb! Get to know some basic information about your particular corner of the Southeast. Learn the average low and high temperatures (which translate into cold hardiness and heat tolerance), as well as the soil type, to make wise plant choices for your garden.

Perhaps the ultimate source of inspiration and information comes when you see a plant in its native haunts and learn what conditions it requires. Every state has a native plant society that plans field trips to interesting habitats across its state. Join your society, go on the trips, find out who is most knowledgeable, and ask them questions. You will learn a lot and see sights that thrill you. The more people who know and appreciate native plants and their habitats, the more plants we can preserve for future generations to enjoy.

THE NAMES OF NATIVE PLANTS

A rose by any other name may be fine in love, but when it comes to gardening, knowing just which kind of rose you're planting matters. Mix up multiflora with swamp and you've just chosen an exotic invasive over a native species. The plant profiles in this book are arranged alphabetically by scientific name within each plant category—so you can see botanical relationships. These names appear first in each listing. However, new gardeners almost always use common names—they are in plain language, familiar, and often colorful or charming. So the plant's common name appears just below the scientific name, in large, prominent, easy-to-read type, for searching by common name. Ironically, common names can lead to misunderstanding. Sometimes two unrelated plants are given the same common name, or a name that is popular in one region is unknown in another. Don't feel bad about using them, but know that at some point, you

may end up buying or talking (or arguing!) about a different plant than you intended. The beauty of using scientific names is that everyone everywhere in the world uses that single name for one specific plant. Unless you took Latin in school, scientific names may seem unfamiliar and cruelly unpronounceable. Our advice to you is to stay calm, keep growing plants, and learn a few scientific names as you go.

Let's break them down. Each species' scientific name consists of two Latin-style words—a noun called the genus, and an adjective called the specific epithet or adjective. Together, they make the species name. For instance, *Lobelia cardinalis* is a species of native plant commonly called cardinal flower. *Lobelia* is the genus and *cardinalis* is the specific adjective. There are other species within the genus *Lobelia*—for instance, *Lobelia spicata* and *Lobelia siphilitica*. Sometimes specific adjectives are informative. In this case, *cardinalis* tells us that the flower is red (like the native bird and Catholic bishops with the same root name).

Have you noticed that plant tags are often longer than two words, though? For instance, *Lobelia cardinalis* 'Queen Victoria'. This name is designating an individual *selection* of the species. Making a comparison, we are all *Homo sapiens*, but Bob from Walhalla is a particular human with his own combination of genes. We would call Bob an individual (boring or bizarre personality aside). With plants, we call this a cultivar—short for "cultivated variety." 'Queen Victoria' is a cultivar of *Lobelia cardinalis* that has dark burgundy foliage. Cultivars are almost always propagated vegetatively to maintain a clone of the original individual. Cultivars, rather than seed-grown species, are the norm in the perennial and woody nursery industry, mainly because they assure uniformity—something we as consumers have been trained to expect.

Check out another plant tag and you may encounter a genus with only a cultivar name, like *Lobelia* 'Monet Moment'. If this name were fully written out, as *Lobelia* × *speciosa* 'Monet Moment', a secret would be revealed. The "×" means this is a hybrid. Two or more different species of *Lobelia* were crossbred, then a particularly desirable

Cardinal flower (*Lobelia cardinalis*) is one of many southeastern natives celebrated by gardeners everywhere.

individual was chosen, named, and propagated to produce many plants of the same genetic makeup. Hybrids might be between different native species of the same genus, or could be hybrids of exotic species of the same genus, or a mixture of the two.

A more recent trend is that of giving cultivars or a group of related cultivars trademarked names, such as Lobelia Fan® Scarlet. The trademarked name is technically not the same as a cultivar name and is not a part of the plant's scientific designation. However, for the consumer, that's splitting hairs. If you buy a Lobelia Fan® Scarlet, you are still buying a hybrid *Lobelia* cultivar (but with that name hidden). Why have plant breeders dropped listing the cultivar in favor of

trademarked names? That could be a chapter unto itself, but it boils down to propriety (control of propagation and supply of the plant) and marketing.

All this decoding of names and selections and hybrids is like seeing how the sausage is made. Perhaps you'd rather just enjoy that gorgeous plant that draws in the humming-birds. But for others, this is important consumer information, necessary to fully understand the history and genetics of the plant being added to your garden. It allows you to look up additional information and learn about the plant's origins. If you are the former, plant it and enjoy (just keep the plant tag)! If you'd like to dig deeper, read on.

Once we've stepped outside the field of naturally reproducing plants, and into cultivars and hybrids, our simple definition of native could cause some head-scratching. If a particular individual of a native species has been found or bred, then propagated and named in the past 150 years, is it still native? "Nativar" is a recently made-up term to refer to just such a cultivar of a native species—*Lobelia cardinalis* 'Queen Victoria', for instance. Opinions among experts vary, but we think of nativars as native plants because the species are native. For us, 'Queen Victoria' cardinal flower is a native plant. Some nativars are selections that look very much like a typical example of that species and provide all the usual features and resources of that species. Others can be quite different—for example, double-flowered types, which may provide less or no nectar or seeds.

Stepping into hybrid territory, things can get a bit stickier. We embrace hybrids of native species, even if they don't occur freely in the wild, and refer to them as "native hybrids." There are some wonderful garden plants that are hybrids between native and exotic species of the same genus, but we can't rightly call them native. We still grow and enjoy them, though, as long as they show no signs of becoming invasive.

While we take a liberal view of "native" when it comes to a home garden, there are definitely applications where stricter definitions should rule. Seed from open-pollinated species, rather than nativars and hybrids, are critical for large-scale conservation and restoration projects where the genetic makeup of reproducing populations is a central concern. Deciding which cultivar or straight species belongs in your garden, however, is a personal decision based on your reasons for choosing natives in the first place. Does the cultivar still provide the same degree of food and shelter for native pollinators or birds? Once established, does it grow without excess inputs and not take over the garden? Is it beautiful, reminiscent of a favorite habitat, or just bring you joy? If any or all of these reasons, or your own reasons, are satisfied, we encourage you to grow it with abandon.

Garden As Habitat

Biodiversity is the key to maintenance of the world as we know it. —E.O. WILSON

A **garden** is generally defined as a planned space, usually outdoors, set aside for the display, cultivation, or enjoyment of plants and other forms of nature. A **habitat** is the type of natural environment in which a particular species of organism lives and finds food, shelter, and protection, and mates for reproduction. Gardens are grown by people, but does that mean they aren't natural? Can a garden be an environment where species find their necessities? In other words, can a garden be a habitat?

We are a part of nature, even as we impact our environment in dramatic ways, and our gardens contain living organisms of all sorts, some of which find all the elements of home. So while gardens aren't and cannot duplicate wild habitat, they certainly *can* provide basic needs for a variety of species if we make wise choices of what goes in them. As Claudia West, coauthor of *Planting in a Post-Wild World*, reminds us, the "wild" we think is outside our cities is mostly gone. It's time to embrace the nature around (and within) us and use what we know to build healthier, more ecologically functional landscapes. It may not be perfect, but it's what we've got and it's something each of us can influence. Even if you narrow your focus to the view outside your window, aren't more butterflies and birds a sight for weary eyes?

Boosting the function of your landscape is not complicated—at the heart of it is diversity and an easing back from harsh interventions. The foundation is a landscape with layers of ground cover, perennials, shrubs, and trees consisting of a variety of at least 50 percent native species. Add to that a basin of water, avoidance of pesticides, and keeping some organic matter in place, and you've covered the basics. Such a garden habitat will contain pollinators, dispersers, beneficial as well as pest insects, reptiles, mammals, and countless unseen players like fungi, bacteria, and micro-invertebrates. Knowing that all players belong

Home gardens come alive when they are made up of at least 50 percent native plants, provide habitat that offers water and organic matter, and are as free of pesticides as possible.

and contribute to a healthy community means that seeing a black snake might make your skin crawl (or tingle with joy), but you allow it. You'll soon realize it's not a sign of a problem, it's a sign of balance—unless roaming rodents are at the top of your wish list.

Of course, even with our best efforts, a reasonable balance isn't always possible. Anyone with deer pressure knows this all too well. You will experience challenges. It might not be deer parties in the backyard, but it could be hungry rabbits, voles, or a particular insect infestation. Whatever the challenge, seek the advice of other gardeners or the local extension service. Consider their advice with the home habitat in mind when you decide if and what action you will take. It's like we tell our young children, does the size of your reaction fit the size of your problem? Especially give

serious thought before using broad-spectrum insecticides. If you spray one, you spray them all.

The three Bs

Birds, butterflies, and bees are just three types of garden visitors or residents, but for us they are joy on the wing, and a stroll through the garden without them lacks dimension. If your answer to the three Bs is "Yes, please!", then get to know their basic needs and fine-tune with their preferences. They all require sources of food, shelter from harsh conditions and predators, nesting or breeding sites, water, and to avoid deadly poisons. Native plants can provide the first three, sometimes the fourth, and you can control the last two.

BIRDS

Adult backyard birds have varied diets, but they center on fruits, seeds, and insects. Baby birds, on the other hand, are only fed insects, caterpillars particularly. What do hungry caterpillars eat? Plants, of course, and often specific native ones (see sidebar). Research by Dr. Doug Tallamy and others continues to show that native plants, especially trees, support a higher diversity and volume of insect larvae than non-natives. He has extended his research to measuring the impact that availability of caterpillars in an urban environment have on chickadee populations and the results are startling. We encourage you to read some of these studies yourself to understand why he compares each plant in your landscape to a feeder. Whether it is full or empty comes down to native vs. non-native in most cases. Don't panic, just plant more natives.

Year-round residents and migrating birds depend on seasonal fruits (see sidebar). Growing plants with summer fruit like serviceberry and plants with winter fruit like dogwoods will boost your avian café star rating. While providing seeds in feeders is fine, don't miss the opportunity to observe goldfinches dining au naturel on yellow coneflower seed heads. Wait until birds have had a chance to pick clean the seeds of coneflowers, sunflowers, asters, mountain mints, and ornamental grasses before cutting them back. Likewise, keep your leaf litter on site. Rake it under shrubs or on seasonal beds and you'll enjoy watching brown thrashers kicking around for insects hiding underneath.

Some birds nest high in trees, others in dense shrubs, and a few on the ground. Making sure your landscape has a variety of foliage layers provides for them all. Some birds nest in cavities of dead trees, something most one-fifth acre lots (or townhouse patios!) can't sustain, so nesting boxes on poles are a great substitute. A few evergreens mixed into your landscape means favorite winter shelter spots for birds. Brush piles are great cover, as well. We've seen them built artistically to please both the birds and the neighbors. Finally, don't forget a source of water, like a birdbath, especially in times of drought or frozen ground. If this sounds like a lot to consider, just go back to the principle of variety over too much uniformity, and reduce your maintenance by not over-tidying. You will end up checking many of these boxes without a complicated to-do list.

The Southeast claims one native species of hummingbird—the ruby-throated. Hummingbirds consume flower nectar and tree sap as a source of energy, along with spiders and tiny insects for adult protein and baby food. From the early red buckeye and columbine to the summer cardinal flower and trumpet creeper to fall salvias, native plants are the original feeders for these zippy wonders. Fill your garden with seasonal species (see sidebar) and you'll be roused from your weeding by the whirr of wings and maybe even an eye-to-eye experience.

An eastern bluebird enjoys the early fall berries of a flowering dogwood (*Cornus florida*).

Shallow basins of water are welcoming to birds such as this eastern towhee.

Shrubs and Trees with Seasonal Fruit for Birds

SUMMER	FALL	WINTER
blackberries (*Rubus*)	American strawberry-bush (*Euonymus americanus*)	Carolina cherry-laurel (*Prunus caroliniana*)
black cherry (*Prunus serotina*)	beautyberry (*Callicarpa americana*)	chokeberries (*Aronia*)
blueberries (*Vaccinium*)	black gum (*Nyssa sylvatica*)	common wax-myrtle (*Morella cerifera*)
elderberry (*Sambucus canadensis*)	dogwoods (*Cornus*)	eastern red cedar (*Juniperus virginiana*)
serviceberries (*Amelanchier*)	fringe tree (*Chionanthus virginicus*)	hollies (*Ilex*)
	spicebush (*Lindera benzoin*)	sumacs (*Rhus*)
	magnolias (*Magnolia*)	
	smooth witherod (*Viburnum nudum*)	

Hummingbirds rely on flowers such as those of trumpet creeper (*Campsis radicans*) for nectar.

BUTTERFLIES AND BEES

Birds are dispersers of seed and hummingbirds are pollinators, but the real workhorses of pollination in our region are bees and butterflies (with nods to flies, beetles, and moths, as well).

Much has been written about the types of flowers that bees and butterflies prefer for foraging nectar and pollen. Clusters of tubular blooms or large flat blooms with an area for landing, in shades of purple, red, orange, and yellow are classically associated with butterflies. Fragrant, blue or yellow, two-lipped flowers or bowl-shaped flowers have been called favorites of bees. These patterns, called pollination syndromes, are intriguing, but far from rules. Many flowers are visited by bees, butterflies, and hummingbirds alike. Do your own study of the visitors to particular flowers in your garden, especially if you've got kids to enlist. It's great fun to notice patterns and to make your own discoveries.

Swamp titi (*Cyrilla racemiflora*) is a pollinator magnet in the Southeast.

To provide a steady flow of nectar for adult bees and butterflies, pick a mixture of early-, mid-, and late-blooming species (see sidebar on page 26). For perennials, groupings of three or more of the same species are attractive to foragers. Adult butterflies and moths can get nectar and pollen from both native and non-native plants, but are quite selective when choosing a plant to feed the next generation. Most require native host plants as food for their caterpillars. Including a few in your garden means those butterflies are not just casual visitors, they've found a home. In times of drought, provide water in a shallow dish half-filled with stones to keep them from having to roam in search of hydration.

Insects need shelter from predators and the elements, and once again, layers in the landscape will provide this. European honeybees raise their young in large colonies, but most native bees are solitary and raise their offspring in dead trees, branches, hollow stems, or sandy soils. Brush piles can provide nesting sites, but may not fit your or your HOA's aesthetics. It's not complicated to create some nifty-looking nesting sites, if you choose. Browse the web for inspiration, and consult the Xerces Society website for up-to-date specifics on construction.

Caterpillar Host Plants

There are many native plants, including species that aren't considered ornamental, that feed the larval stage of butterflies and moths. Some of these pairings are very specific, such as the famous monarch–milkweed relationship. Others are broader, like the eastern tiger swallowtail, whose caterpillars can feed on different trees such as cherries, magnolias, birches, and willows. The following is just a sampling of ornamental host plants and the charismatic butterflies whose caterpillars they feed. We include poplars and willows in this list because they are host to many caterpillars. They are not included in the 225 recommendations because they are rarely planted as ornamentals.

One of the ways native plants support pollinators is by providing food for the larval (caterpillar) stage of butterflies, such as this spicebush swallowtail (the large eyespots are for protection and are not actual eyes!).

HERBACEOUS HOST PLANT	BUTTERFLY AND MOTH CATERPILLAR
asters (*Symphyotrichum*)	pearl crescent, silvery checkerspot
false indigo (*Baptisia*)	eastern tailed-blue, frosted elfin, clouded sulfur + more
golden Alexander (*Zizia aurea*)	black swallowtail
grasses (many species)	common wood nymph, Carolina satyr, little wood-satyr
milkweed (*Asclepias*)	monarch, queen
pussytoes (*Antennaria*)	American lady
sedges (*Carex*)	a variety of skippers, Appalachian brown
sunflowers (*Helianthus*)	checkerspots, painted lady, giant leopard moth

VINES

American wisteria (*Wisteria frutescens*)	long-tailed skipper
maypops (*Passiflora incarnata*)	variegated fritillary, gulf fritillary
pipevine (*Aristolochia*)	pipevine swallowtail

SHRUBS

blueberries (*Vaccinium*)	striped hairstreak, spring azure, brown elfin
dogwoods (*Cornus*)	spring azure, summer azure
pawpaw (*Asimina triloba*)	zebra swallowtail
serviceberries (*Amelanchier*)	red-spotted purple
spicebush (*Lindera benzoin*)	spicebush swallowtail
viburnums (*Viburnum*)	hummingbird clearwing, spring azure

TREES

birch (*Betula*)	host to more than 350 types of caterpillars
black cherry (*Prunus serotina*)	host to more than 350 types of caterpillars
oak (*Quercus*)	host to more than 350 types of caterpillars
poplar (*Populus*)	host to more than 350 types of caterpillars
willow (*Salix*)	host to more than 350 types of caterpillars

Nectar Plants for Pollinators by Season

Many plants can provide nectar for pollinators, but some are like magnets, drawing winged ones in from afar. We've organized them by early, middle, and late season, so that if you choose one or more from each column, you'll provide one-stop, spring-through-fall sipping.

NECTAR-RICH PERENNIALS FOR BUTTERFLIES AND BEES

Early Season	Mid-Season	Late Season
beardtongues (*Penstemon*)	coneflowers (*Rudbeckia* and *Echinacea*), tickseeds (*Coreopsis*)	ageratums (*Conoclinium*), white snakeroot (*Ageratina*)
bluestars (*Amsonia*)	gayfeather (*Liatris spicata*)	asters (*Symphyotrichum*), goldenrods (*Solidago*)
mouse-ear coreopsis (*Coreopsis auriculata*)	milkweed (*Asclepias*)	hibiscus (*Hibiscus*), seashore mallow (*Kosteletskya pentacarpos*)
phlox (*Phlox stolonifera, P. divaricata, P. carolina*)	mountain mints (*Pycnanthemum*), bee-balm (*Monarda*)	ironweed (*Vernonia*)
robin's-plantain (*Erigeron pulchellus*)	rattlesnake master (*Eryngium yuccifolium*)	Joe-pye weeds (*Eutrochium*)
Stokes' aster (*Stokesia laevis*)	summer phlox (*Phlox paniculata*)	sunflowers (*Helianthus*)

NECTAR-RICH SHRUBS FOR BUTTERFLIES AND BEES

Early Season	Mid-Season	Late Season
native azaleas (*Rhododendron*)	coastal sweet-pepperbush (*Clethra alnifolia*)	elderberries (*Sambucus canadensis*), when reblooms
ninebark (*Physocarpus opulifolius*)	bottlebrush buckeye (*Aesculus parviflora*)	swamp azalea (*Rhododendron viscosum*)
Virginia-willow (*Itea virginica*)	buttonbush (*Cephalanthus occidentalis*)	
	hydrangeas (*Hydrangea*)	
	St. John's wort (*Hypericum*)	

NATURAL HUMMINGBIRD FEEDERS

Early Season	Mid-Season	Late Season
eastern columbine (*Aquilegia canadensis*)	bee-balm (*Monarda*)	jewelweed (*Impatiens capensis*)
coral honeysuckle (*Lonicera sempervirens*)	cardinal flower (*Lobelia cardinalis*)	scarlet sage (*Salvia coccinea*)
cross-vine (*Bignonia capreolata*)	coral bean (*Erythrina herbacea*)	
red buckeye (*Aesculus pavia*)	Indian-pink (*Spigelia marilandica*)	
	trumpet creeper (*Campsis radicans*)	

Pesticide pause

Creating a backyard habitat means more caterpillars for baby birds and more pollinators buzzing about. The goal is to have beneficial insects, as well, to compete with pest and invasive insects. A lively garden will have chewed leaves and sometimes outbreaks of pests. As humans, we are wired to use tools, and some of the most powerful, far-reaching tools of our age are chemicals, so it's an understandable reflex to turn to pesticides when we think we have a problem. But using broad-spectrum insecticides in a habitat we've worked to create makes little sense. It is nearly impossible to avoid poisoning or harming beneficial and pollinator species along with the ones we call pests. Additionally, you may have concerns for unknown effects on other species, including ours.

An alternative to reaching first for pesticides is an approach called integrated pest management (IPM). You can also call it common sense—beginning with the least-toxic approaches to pest problems and only resorting to toxins, if you choose, when there is a catastrophic-level threat. If you're alarmed by what looks like a pest or disease in your garden, take a deep breath and work through this sequence.

1. **Correct identification.** Be sure you know exactly what you're dealing with. Don't skip this step—you'd hate to wipe out a nice population of beneficial insects thinking they are pests. The app *iNaturalist* (for insects), the local extension service, or a Google image search can help.

2. **Level of problem.** Take a reality check and assess whether or not you are dealing with an infestation or just the willies over weird insects on a plant or two.

3. **Can you use a mechanical control?** In other words, can you utilize strong sprays of water to knock off or damage the pests (there are nozzles designed for this), or hand-pick and destroy them?

4. **Is there a less-toxic or narrowly targeted toxin you can use?** Less-toxic options include horticultural soap, oil, or homemade pepper or garlic sprays. Targeted toxins are ones that are specific to a particular pest, such as *Bacillus thuringiensis* for caterpillars.

5. **Educate yourself.** If you are dealing with a crisis and choose to use broad-acting toxins, take extra time to learn more before you spray. Xerces.org is a good place to start for information on how to minimize damage to other insects, such as spraying at night in dry, windless conditions.

Extend your community

Building a backyard habitat on the foundation of native plants is empowering. When you see the rewards, such as more birds and butterflies, you're likely to want to spread the news. One way is to go old school with a habitat certification sign that communicates to neighbors and visitors that your garden isn't just beautiful, it's functionally rich. The National Wildlife Federation, the Audubon Society, and the Million Pollinator Garden Challenge have well-known national home habitat certification programs, but there are also state and local organizations, like native plant societies, that have programs. Local efforts build pride and can spread from neighbor to neighbor.

You can even connect with scientists and contribute to national or global data-sharing projects through backyard bird counts, bioblitzes, City Nature Challenges, and *iNaturalist* app submissions. Search for any of these terms to explore your options. *The Field Guide to Citizen Science* (2020) and scistarter.org share numerous ways for home gardeners to participate in important field research. Build it, watch them come, enjoy it, and don't keep it a secret. Micro-habitats become stronger together.

Can you find the Carolina anole lizard hidden in this red chokeberry (*Aronia arbutifolia*)?

Plant Selection

Whether you're a plan-first or plant-forward kind of person, starting or building upon a garden is an exciting endeavor abuzz with imagination, hope, and sometimes fear. *I can't wait to see it bloom! Will my plan look like I imagine? Is this the best plant for this spot? I hope I can keep it alive!* Use your excitement to your advantage by backing it up with some forethought and patience, and you've got nothing to fear.

It's easy to focus entirely on the plant when it's time to go shopping. A visit to the garden center or online nursery can be like online dating. You're surrounded by pretty faces, and the descriptions make them sound too good to be true. On your way to the register, you suddenly wonder, *Can I trust this plant?* Put that voice to rest with an age-old match-making secret: accurate knowledge. If you take a moment to understand three things—your site, yourself, and the plants—you may rest assured that this relationship is starting on solid ground. Picking native plants is no different than picking any plant. Every plant has both limits and potential, every site has particular light and soil conditions, and every gardener has a personality that translates into desires. The bulk of this book is about understanding the plants, so this section focuses on your site and yourself.

Site smarts

It all begins with light. Describing garden light requires taking a plant's perspective and is not an exact science. From season to season and daily as the sun moves across the sky, light varies in the same spot. Sun, shade, part sun, part shade, high shade, filtered light, open shade, morning sun—what do they all mean? We use a four-category system, ranging from low to high light: shade, part shade (which includes open shade and high shade), part sun (includes filtered sun), and sun.

Sun means full sun for at least seven hours, including afternoon sun. This is good for grasses, meadow and

Once you identify the types of light in your garden, you can match plants to their light preferences.

roadside plants, many nectar-bearing pollinator plants, and aquatic and marsh plants. Plants have to be tough to take the full brunt of the afternoon sun, tolerating the stress of less water available during hot temperatures. Some plants require full sun, many tolerate it, some suffer from it. If a plant is listed as accepting both full sun and part shade, it means it would appreciate some relief from the afternoon sun. If you must give full sun, keeping the soil moist may prevent scorched leaves. Species native to the northern ends of our region definitely prefer some afternoon shade when they're planted farther south.

Part sun means morning to midday sun only, with afternoon protection. Plants in part sun may still see some open sky in the afternoon, but direct sun does not warm the leaves for long. The eastern or northern side of a house without nearby trees gives good part sun conditions, as does a garden open to sun but surrounded by tall trees around the periphery. In such places, there is abundant light, but not direct sun all day. Some plants that prefer full sun can still grow well in such sites.

Part shade means the plant is under high shade from tall trees, with few low limbs and no dense understory trees. There are openings in the canopy where sun can come in, but never for so long that plant leaves heat up. Part shade can be called open shade, filtered shade, or high shade. It is ideal for most woodland plants that never grow in direct sun.

Shade means full shade. Plants in shade hardly get a ray of direct sunlight. Deep shade is found under a dense canopy of low limbs. Many woodland plants are adapted to these conditions, however, they may perform even better when in part shade. Ferns are ideal in deep shade since they do not bloom. If you have deep shade, removing a few saplings or lower branches can transform shade to part shade and expand your plant choices for that area.

Be accurate in assessing your light and respect the light needs of different species. Placing plants according to their sun needs and tolerances is at the heart of the "right plant, right place" mantra and goes further than any other factor in determining long-term success.

Soil is the other foundation of site. Many of the plants in this book are tolerant of a range of soil types, and evaluating your soil is covered in the next chapter. Once you get a feel for what soil type you have, you'll start to learn which plants do the very best in your conditions. Some plants will require well-drained conditions, and there is no wiggle room there. If you have heavy clay, choose a different plant.

You've looked up and down, now look around. One of the easiest mistakes to make is to put a plant in a spot without room for expansion. Just drive around a subdivision that's ten years old and check out the plants swallowing up windows. Don't judge a plant by the size it is in the container you buy. Read and believe the height and spread dimensions listed in its description. Those reflect a ten-year average. In planning, take note of how much room the new plant will realistically have in its new home. In areas next to a walkway or door, pay particular attention to this, as well as avoiding plants with thorns, messy fruit, or (if it's a concern) bee-magnet flowers.

The plan advantage

We wouldn't be doing our jobs if we didn't advise beginning with some sort of plan, but we'd be lying if we said we'd never (okay, often) come home from the garden center with plants we fell in love with, but had no idea where those plants would go. It tends to work out alright as long as we respect the needs of the plants and realistically match those needs to our sites. The plants grow and we learn what we like and what we don't.

If you have an established landscape with which you're content, adding native plants is just a matter of finding empty spots, beds to expand, or plants you'd like to replace. If you're starting a sizable area—or an entire landscape—from scratch, you need a plan on paper. There are simple books, online resources, and design professionals to guide you. Delving into principles of design is far beyond the scope of this book, but whether you go DIY or work with a designer, it pays to learn a few basic principles. It's fun (and useful) when you realize *why* a particular planting is so pleasing while another is not. A professional plan is by no means a requirement for having a garden you love. If you're starting from a blank slate, require a unified style for your garden, or have serious drainage issues, working with a landscape architect or designer is a worthwhile investment. Know that if you already have a professional plan that calls for mostly exotics, it's no problem to make substitutions with natives that fill similar roles.

If you're going the DIY route, get started by looking for landscapes, in person or virtually, that you love. While viewing one, explain out loud to someone else what it is you notice and like about it. Do this for a few examples and each time, have that person write down what you say. Next, make a list of all the ways you and your family use your outdoor space or would like to use it.

Now that you are warmed up, zero in. Like beginning any new relationship, it can be tempting to lose yourself in the fantasy. Bring things back to reality by asking yourself, *If this plant or planting could only accomplish two things, what would they be?* Those answers might be practical or idiosyncratic—it doesn't matter, as long as they are the two most important factors to you in this spot. Examples include providing flowers for pollinators, blocking a view, casting shade, matching your house, or feeding birds with berries. By zeroing in on two, you'll make a choice that satisfies for the long run.

The Mellichamp Natives Terrace at the University of North Carolina Charlotte Botanical Gardens honors Larry's 40-year career as the Gardens' director, and features a wide variety of southeastern natives on display for homeowners.

A plan may be a simple list of needs or a detailed sketch. It's not necessary to nail down species yet, but a list of potential options is helpful. Focus on what you want each area of the landscape to accomplish, and note the light conditions and relative space available. For instance, you might draw a circle and write "screen this view, part shade conditions, 25 ft. × 4 ft." or "pollinator planting, almost full sun, 8 ft. × 6 ft." The point of a plan is to keep you moving forward without having to rethink and remind yourself of basic decisions and givens. Never forget that your garden is a living space—embrace it as a place to reflect what brings you joy and fulfills your needs. Plans are there to revisit as both you and your garden change over time.

In creating a plan or thinking about additions, having names for traditional landscape elements is helpful. But know that you are not limited by these categories. If you are not restricted, you may want to experiment with different styles, like a minimalistic contemporary style or a naturalistic style that takes direct inspiration from regional plant communities and embraces seasonal changes in an evolving landscape.

Foundation plants are generally evergreen shrubs that fit near the house to give it a context, hide the ground, soften the corners, and border the windows. The usual exotic suspects planted by builders, such as Asian hollies, are chosen for their low cost and indestructibility. But they are often

Fringe tree in full bloom is an example of a good southeastern specimen plant.

inappropriate in scale and require pruning several times a year. Instead, choose something whose ultimate size is manageable with little to no pruning. Dwarf evergreen native plant choices are limited, but function over flair tends to be their *raison d'etre*, anyway. Dwarf forms of yaupon holly, inkberry holly, common wax-myrtle, and Walter's viburnum are prime choices for a sunny foundation. Foundations don't have to be uniform masses of green meatballs or loaves, either. We enjoy a mix of dwarf shrubs and perennials, or grasses that shine spring through fall. We don't mind a couple winter months of relative bareness.

Specimen plants stand alone in the landscape to show off their superior qualities. Generally, they are striking shrubs or small trees that offer beauty for two or more seasons and improve with age. For example, Japanese maples

are classic exotic specimen plants. Flowering dogwood, red buckeye, southern magnolia, two-winged silverbell, and river birch are examples of native specimen plants.

Accent plants have one or more better-than-average traits, such as showy flowers or colorful berries. They are often used in mixed borders, islands, near hardscape, or in groupings where you want a pop of interest. Accent plants can be shrubs, select perennials, ornamental grasses, or small trees. Think beautyberry, hydrangeas, coastal sweet-pepperbush, scarlet hibiscus, purple coneflower, and muhly grass.

Property border plants can be shrubs, large grasses, or trees planted along a straight or curving edge of a property, demarcating or screening. They may blend in or provide a seasonal showcase. A mixed border has plants of similar sizes and growth rates, yet each brings a different feature to the mix. Hedges are borders of one species grown close together and pruned regularly to create a living wall. If you crave formality, hedges deliver. You must prune a hedge wider at the bottom, narrower at the top, so the lower branches receive enough sunlight to remain leafy. Privacy screens are a form of taller hedge, generally at least 15 ft., often not requiring pruning. They are visual fences, so unless you don't mind your fence disappearing in winter, choose an evergreen.

Flower border plants are grown together to delight the senses with colorful blooms and are mainly perennials and annuals, although ornamental grasses steal the show in contemporary plantings. If you want to maximize pollinator activity, go for a variety of early-, mid-, and late-season bloomers. Many of our natives are staples of perennial gardens across the temperate world: beardtongue, coreopsis, phlox, milkweed, bee-balm, coneflower, aster, and goldenrod. A mixed border in this context refers to a combination of shrubs and perennials or ornamental grasses.

Ground covers are low-growing plants that occupy space, filling in areas that otherwise would have bare soil, mulch, or lawn. They can be ground hugging or slightly taller. Evergreens are desirable, but deciduous species are used as well. Because they are valued for growing rapidly and spreading, some of the most popular exotic ground covers have become invasive—English ivy, winter creeper, and vinca, for instance. Native ground covers such as green-and-gold spread more slowly and don't choke out their neighbors.

Shade trees are tall and long lived. They are invaluable, yet most homeowners don't have the opportunity to choose them, as they were either left on the property during construction (becoming rarer) or planted early on to provide shade for the future. The good news is that almost all the best and most often-used shade trees, such as most oaks and maples, are native. They are visual and ecological anchors in the garden. If you have the chance to plant your own, choose a spot that won't crowd others or be too near the house.

Lawns are planted expanses of a single species of grass, traditionally intensively maintained through weekly mowing to a short, uniform profile. Valued for their restful, uniform appearance and functionality as children's play areas, they carry cultlike status among many homeowners. There is just one native species of lawn grass for the Southeast: St. Augustine grass.

Despite their ubiquity and fan base, lawns have drawbacks, especially when we understand the value of our yards as living contributors to the web of life. A traditionally grown lawn sucks up resources—water to keep it green, chemical pesticides and fertilizers to grow it like a crop, gasoline to run mowers and aerators. What we end up with, however pleasing to the eye, is not food, but a food desert. A monoculture of grass contributes very little to other creatures. That may be hard to wrap your head around. Something so ingrained in our culture is not going to disappear anytime soon and you may value your lawn so highly that you wouldn't want it to. But just like mixing natives and non-natives, this doesn't have to be an either/or decision. Instead, you could choose to reduce the size of your lawn and take a more balanced approach to its maintenance. When you run out of room in your beds for trying new native plants, look to your lawn. Carve out a new bed or move existing beds out a foot or so each year. However, the easiest way to bring more life to your lawn is to simply allow it to become a mix of species rather than one grass, and end the inputs of toxins and extra water. This also has the advantage of saving money. Clover, dandelions, sedges, and plantain mixed with grasses are just as mowable and make a fine field for soccer drills. Early blooms of those (before the mower comes out) feed pollinators, the leaves feed butterfly larvae, and clover adds nitrogen to the soil. No, you won't have a perfect green carpet—rather, a living quilt that gives something back. Peer pressure can be strong, homeowner associations (HOAs) even stronger, but it's time to start the conversation. We're in this together.

Speaking of HOAs, if your landscape decisions are subject to their guidelines, this does not mean you have to use exotic plants. Native plants can be used in traditional-style

landscapes. Often guidelines have more to do with maintenance than plant species restriction. We love to see the natural form of plants, but a hedged native holly has as many habitat benefits as an unpruned one. Read the guidelines of your HOA and if you feel they are overly restrictive, especially if they dictate certain species and impact your ability to make sustainable and eco-wise choices, appeal to the board. In a spirit of improving your community, share with them the benefits of both native plants and sustainable landscape practices such as less water usage, pollinator support, and fewer toxins added to the neighborhood.

You may find yourself without access to much of a yard, with or without a lawn. You can still grow plants, even a few native ones. Container and dish gardens can adorn a partially sunny patio or a balcony. Obviously, there are limits to what can be grown in containers, but we've enjoyed success with part shade perennial combinations like heucheras, ferns, and sedges. A mini–pollinator garden of dwarf coneflower, threadleaf coreopsis, and mealycup sage makes a lively show in a large, sunny container.

One last type of garden that you may be curious about is a meadow. The idea of a mixed grass and wildflower meadow is glorious and carefree. The reality of creating one is, ironically, very high maintenance. Botanical gardens and others are experimenting with creating meadows and the successful ones are fabulous, but they are not something the majority of home gardeners are prepared to undertake. Thankfully, the word is mostly out that "meadow in a can" is not any sort of sustainable garden solution. Many of the species in these mixes are not native, even though they are often referred to as wildflowers, and when you clear ground to spread the seeds, it means many more than the canned ones will sprout. Weeds love a clear spot. Meadow seed mixes are best used as something fun for kids to play with in small raised beds, to see what will grow in one short season.

Temperatures

The Southeast is a great place for gardening, with its mild winters and gradual change of seasons. The region is far from uniform, however, as reflected in a range of hardiness zones from 6 to 9, with the high mountains much colder than the coastal lowlands.

The numbers following "Z" that you'll find on any plant tag are the USDA hardiness zones. Hardiness is defined as the ability of a plant to withstand cold winter temperatures. While listed as a range, such as "zone 7–10", the lower number is key, indicating that the plant can't survive the average winter anywhere north of zone 7.

But it's not cold winters that are the climate extreme of most concern in the Southeast, it's the scorching hot summers. It's important to understand that plants from mountain zones in the Southeast are not always heat tolerant. We rarely lose native plants in the ground to cold. During the summer, however, when night temperatures are above 70°F for long periods (usually two months or more), a plant in the Southeast is forced to use more energy during its nighttime rest period. This uses up stored energy that would otherwise go into growing and flowering. Plants that evolved in the hotter regions of the Southeast are adapted to this, but others waste away or "melt" in the heat, as some southerners say. This situation is counterintuitive, because we have been conditioned by older books and plant information tags to believe that the only temperature limitation to worry about is cold hardiness.

Both cold and heat tolerances vary from plant to plant within a species, based on where the selected plant originated. A single species that grows widely from Maine to Florida, such as red maple (*Acer rubrum*), will be differently adapted at one end of its range than at the other. This hasn't always been well understood in the horticulture industry, and has resulted in northern-selected plants being sold in the south to less than stellar results. Awareness of this,

◄ To create a border that offers plenty of color during warm months, choose native perennials.

Native species of black-eyed Susan (*Rudbeckia*), beach blanket flower (*Gaillardia*), and bee-balm (*Monarda*) bring this meadow to life in summer.

called plant provenance, is greater now. It never hurts to do a quick Google search on a particular species, adding "for the Southeast" to identify any best-bet cultivars or ones to avoid.

Southern plants can be taken up north with some success, but northern and high-mountain plants cannot be brought into the hot Southeast, in many cases. You can alter a site by adding shade, modifying the soil, and providing more water, but you can't make it cooler at night. The solution to this problem is to obtain plants from southern sources when possible. For instance, given the choice to order a bloodroot from Georgia or Wisconsin, always choose the former.

Because zones refer to cold hardiness, not heat tolerance, you need to understand that zone 8 in Portland, Oregon, may be the same temperature in winter as zone 8 in Portland, Alabama, but the summers are very different. Plants such as garden delphinium that thrive on the west coast won't last a week in July down south.

The American Horticultural Society produced a heat-zone map to help gardeners understand the effects of heat on plant growth, but it has never been formally adopted by the industry. However, the heat zones will often match up with the higher number of the cold hardiness zones. If a plant is hardy in Zones 4–7, it is a good clue that it will likely suffer in the summers of zones 8 and 9.

Finding native plants

By now, you're probably more than ready to go plant shopping. You know what you want, you just need to know where to find it. You've got several options, depending on the sizes and species you're seeking. Local garden centers and big box stores tend to carry the most common natives that are mass-produced on a national scale, primarily perennials like orange butterfly-weed, coneflower, and phlox. If the stores have knowledgeable staff, ask what natives they carry. If selections are limited, request that they offer more. You won't be alone. Specialty nurseries are well worth seeking out and supporting (you'll miss them when they are gone). They grow and sell a much wider range of natives, often with options for both on-site purchases and mail order (see resources). Get to know the staff, establish a relationship,

Flame azalea (*Rhododendron calendulaceum*) prefers the cooler, wetter climate of the Southeast's high country.

and encourage them to grow new species that are of interest to you. While a Google search for "native plant nurseries" is a great start, you may miss some local gems. Just be sure they have a clear statement or pledge that they do not collect from the wild and only sell nursery-propagated material.

Most native plant societies have lists of native plant nurseries on their websites, as well as botanical gardens with a focus on natives. Botanical garden plant sales can be excellent sources of native plants, so find out dates, mark your calendar, and look forward to their special selections.

Another way to acquire plants, along with knowledge and friends, is by joining a regional or state plant society—every southeastern state has one. The North Carolina Native Plant Society, for example, is the oldest regional plant society in the country and has two annual plant auctions to raise money, as well as a seed exchange. Individuals bring common and rare plants they have propagated, and the fun begins.

Some individual growers offer native plants on eBay. Be careful when buying plants you can't see—they may not be alive or they could be the wrong plant. Unfortunately, some plant sellers buy natives cheaply from local collectors who dig the plants from the wild and sell them as is. This results in impoverished plant communities, millions of plants dying from improper care, and people throwing their money away. Do not buy cheap plants from dealers you do not know; the real cost is far too high.

Special Garden Needs

Some gardens have special needs. If you have a challenging spot to fill, consider the following suggestions.

RAIN GARDEN OR PERIODICALLY WET SOIL

buttonbush *(Cephalanthus occidentalis)*

climbing aster *(Ampelaster carolinianus)*

coastal sweet-pepperbush *(Clethra alnifolia)*

cutleaf coneflower *(Rudbeckia laciniata)*

gayfeather *(Liatris spicata)*

Joe-pye weed *(Eutrochium)*

muhly grass *(Muhlenbergia capillaris)*

pond cypress *(Taxodium ascendens)*

river birch *(Betula nigra)*

rose mallow *(Hibiscus moscheutos)*

serviceberry *(Amelanchier)*

St. John's wort *(Hypericum)*

swamp milkweed *(Asclepias incarnata)*

swamp sunflower *(Helianthus angustifolius)*

sweet-bay magnolia *(Magnolia virginiana)*

switch grass *(Panicum virgatum)*

Virginia-willow *(Itea virginica)*

winterberry *(Ilex verticillata)*

HELL-STRIPS (DRY, FULL SUN)

black-eyed Susan *(Rudbeckia hirta)*

butterfly-weed *(Asclepias tuberosa)*

dwarf wax-myrtle *(Morella* 'Don's Dwarf'*)*

dwarf yaupon holly *(Ilex vomitoria* 'Nana'*)*

muhly grass *(Muhlenbergia capillaris)*

switch grass *(Panicum virgatum,* esp. dwarf forms*)*

threadleaf bluestar *(Amsonia hubrichtii)*

Yucca filamentosa

SALT-SPRAY TOLERANT FOR THE BEACH

beach blanket flower *(Gaillardia pulchella)*

cabbage palmetto *(Sabal palmetto)*

Carolina cherry-laurel *(Prunus caroliniana)*

coastal red cedar *(Juniperus virginiana* var. *silicicola)*

common wax-myrtle *(Morella cerifera)*

coral bean *(Erythrina herbacea)*

little bluestem grass *(Schizachyrium scoparium)*

muhly grass *(Muhlenbergia)*

seashore mallow *(Kosteletskya virginica)*

serviceberry *(Amelanchier)*

spotted horsemint *(Monarda punctata)*

yaupon holly *(Ilex vomitoria)*

yucca *(Yucca)*

Fall and Winter Appeal

OUTSTANDING FALL COLOR

Alabama croton *(Croton alabamensis)*

black gum *(Nyssa sylvatica)*

blueberry *(Vaccinium)*

bottlebrush buckeye *(Aesculus parviflora)*

chokeberries *(Aronia)*

dwarf fothergilla *(Fothergilla gardenii)*

flowering dogwood *(Cornus florida)*

maple *(Acer)*

native azalea *(Rhododendron)*

oakleaf hydrangea *(Hydrangea quercifolia)*

persimmon *(Diospyros virginiana)*

sassafras *(Sassafras albidum)*

serviceberries *(Amelanchier)*

smooth witherod *(Viburnum nudum)*

sourwood *(Oxydendrum arboreum)*

sumac *(Rhus)*

threadleaf bluestar *(Amsonia hubrichtii)*

ATTRACTIVE BARK

American strawberry-bush *(Euonymus americanus)*

blueberry *(Vaccinium)*

mountain sweet-pepperbush *(Clethra acuminata)*

oakleaf hydrangea *(Hydrangea quercifolia)*

ninebark *(Physocarpus opulifolius)*

river birch *(Betula nigra)*

striped maple *(Acer pensylvanicum)*

Traffic dividers and hell-strips can be good places for non-thirsty natives that like full sun.

Keep It Growing

One of the biggest hurdles for gardeners is also one of the best things about gardening: it takes time. But it is time well spent that provides a lifetime of potential for creating, learning, and experiencing new fascinations. Not every plant will grow for you like you saw it growing elsewhere, or you may grow something better than anyone else. That is part of the fun—it's about the journey, the challenges and the thrill when things thrive, not necessarily the conclusion. So pace yourself. Some of the best advice we have is to start small. We promise you that delight can come from just one well-grown plant, and your success will be like seeds of motivation to drive you toward your vision.

This is where gardening turns from noun to verb. There are few instantly fatal mistakes in the garden, but plenty of learning opportunities. The act of planting can be exhilarating, and even maintenance like pruning and weeding can be surprisingly satisfying (midday in summertime excluded). You cannot control everything (as in life) and change is at the center of it all. But there is a rhythm as well, and once you decide what level of maintenance suits your temperament, you'll find it. By all means, don't be afraid

Yellow trillium (*Trillium luteum*) and fernleaf phacelia (*Phacelia bipinnatifida*) species prefer spring shade.

to experiment and kill a plant in the process. A dead plant is just nutrients ready for recycling. Enjoy the plants that are growing and shining in your garden and don't fret over those that didn't take root.

If you are a new gardener, take a look at our Quick Start Guide to understand the basic steps of planning to planting. Seasoned gardeners, take a look and reflect on what your experience has been, then get back outside, pull a few weeds, and plan that next bed.

Getting your soil right

You've got some awesome new plants in mind and it's time for shovel to meet soil. Perhaps the least sexy part of gardening is the most important—soil preparation. It all comes down to the roots, the literal foundation of your plants.

Roots must have good contact with soil in order to access water, air, and nutrients. Understanding your soil and how to adjust it is all about those three things. You need to know how soil drains (which relates to water and air) and two key things about its chemistry: can it hold nutrients and what is its pH? Soil pH can be "acidic" (below 6.5) or "basic" (above 7.0). For instance, a very sandy soil with fast drainage provides air, but doesn't hold onto water or nutrients so well. A heavy clay soil holds nutrients and water, but is poorly aerated. A large number of plants thrive in what we call loam, which is somewhere in between those two. The other central component of soil is organic matter or humus. Humus affects the water, air, and nutrients in the soil, in nearly always positive ways. Organic matter feeds the universe of tiny organisms in the soil that bring it to life and result in nutrient release. This is why almost every soil benefits from the additions of organic matter, usually in the form of compost.

New Gardener Quick Start Guide

Dig in the dirt. Grab something to dig with and check out the soil where you'll be planting. If you can get a shovel or trowel down into it in a couple of tries and it isn't pure sand, go on to step 2. Otherwise, you will need to do significant amending or raised bed building (if subsoil clay) first. Seek advice from the extension service or other regional sources. How you create and amend a bed from scratch will vary from region to region due to soil type. This will take time, so plan to do this before planting season.

Stand out in the rain. During or after a heavy rainstorm walk your property and notice where water flows, pools, or scours. If you have major issues, it's best to seek advice from a landscaping contractor or other professional. For minor issues, plan beds to avoid those areas or research a DIY drainage solution.

See the light. Go outside at 9 am, 1 pm, and 4 pm on a sunny, warm-season day in the spot(s) you plan to plant. For each time write down if you are in full sun, bright or dappled shade, or fully in shadow. Use that data to record if your spot is sun, part sun, part shade, or shade.

Think in time and space. Write down the amount of space you have to ultimately fill each gap or new planting. Think in four dimensions – height, depth, spread, and time (plants grow, you know).

Know yourself. Get clear about your needs and desires for your garden and your temperament as a gardener. What are the top three reasons you want a garden? Which pleases you more: a neat and tidy look with clear edges or an abundant, varied, cottage-sort of planting? How much time do you want to spend actually in your garden working? What is your budget? If you determine that a plan is in order, use your answers and data from this and other steps to create (or hire) a plan.

Find your source. Before you are ready to plant, begin locating sources for a variety of native plants. Check out local nurseries, mail order options, and botanical gardens and native plant societies to learn of timing of their plant sales and mark your calendar.

Zero in. For each area you are ready to plant, ask yourself, "if this planting could accomplish just two things, what two are the most important to me?" Make a wish list of plant options or at least the type of plant you're looking for based on your answers. Double check that plant choices fit the light conditions and space available.

Go shopping. It's best to acquire plants close to the time you want to plant them, so you don't have to attend to watering them daily in pots. Fall is best for trees and shrubs. Fall or spring for perennials. Spring for grasses, marginally hardy plants, and annuals.

Prep it. For workable beds, incorporate compost throughout bed, not just in planting holes. If planting in containers, fill with good quality packaged potting soil (not garden soil).

Plant for the long run. Pick a cloudy day or early evening to plant and don't rush. See "planting properly" for details about loosening roots, planting at the right level, getting a firm connection between roots and soil, watering well, and mulching.

Keep things hydrated. Water new plants for one minute, once a week, unless 1 in. of rain. And yes, a beverage in hand and a wide-brimmed straw hat makes this much more pleasant for the gardener, as well.

Raised beds allow gardeners to create soil mixes appropriate for the selections they'll be planting.

As important as soil is, you don't have to figure this out yourself. A search of your regional extension service website will quickly reveal what type of soil you are *likely* to have in your garden, and further searching will lead to advice on how to amend it or build raised beds. Most all have helpline numbers, so call 'em up and chat. If you are seeing yellowish or weak plants in your existing landscape—or just want to know where your soil stands before starting—take advantage of their no- or low-cost soil testing services to learn your soil pH and nutrient levels. A few groups of plants require a more acid soil or abhor it, and are noted in the plant profiles, so it is good to know your pH if considering those plants.

A quick and dirty (unless you wear gloves) way to get the green light on planting in your soil is to attempt to dig a hole. If you can dig down into the soil at least 10 inches, even if it takes a bit of muscle, your soil is workable. Feel it. If you could build a sandcastle with the results, your main challenge will be adding enough organic matter to retain water and nutrients. If the soil forms a clump, but crumbles with a little pressure, you've got some form of loam—a mixture of soil particle sizes with some organic matter. Celebrate. On the other hand, if your trowel made that boingy cartoon sound and bounced back when you tried to dig, you've got clay (or rock), perhaps subsoil.

Unfortunately, clay is what you are likely to encounter in a new development in the Piedmont, and it will require work to improve drainage before it can support more than the toughest trees and shrubs. If you find yourself there with no established beds, we recommend building up. Attempting to work organic matter far down into clay that lacks a topsoil level is challenging and will take several repeated efforts before you see results. It can be done over time, but if you want to get planting immediately, raised beds are the way to go. Seek advice on local sources of good-quality, bulk gardening soil mix from neighborhood gardeners, botanical gardens, or the extension service. Buyer beware: what is called topsoil may sound like the right choice, but in our experience, it almost never is and will frustrate you in the end. This is not the time to cut costs—soil is everything. Likewise, it is very tempting to amend only the holes you dig for plants, rather than the bed or area in general. Don't do it. At best it will delay establishment, at worst your plants won't grow at all. Well-chosen native plants have a long future of relatively low inputs *if* you plant them properly in a uniform soil environment. Native plants in clay-based or loam soils rarely require any fertilizer beyond a yearly topdressing of compost. Plants in sandy soils may benefit from twice-yearly compost or occasional organic fertilizer topdressing.

Good timing

You can prep soil any time of year, but plan to plant or transplant all woody plants in the fall (late September through November). This is also prime time for most perennials and ferns. Fall planting will go far to improve your chances of success because the plants will have three months of moderate temperatures to grow roots to get ready for winter, and then be somewhat established going into their first stressful summer. Spring is best for planting ornamental grasses, marginally hardy species, and annuals. It's also a fine time to plant most perennials and ferns. If you've previously gardened up north, you're used to spring planting everything and plenty of southerners do it, too, but the difference is you must monitor watering and heat stress very closely that first summer. If you're looking to reduce maintenance in the form of watering, opt for fall, especially for woody plants.

Let's plant, already: step by step

1. If possible, pick a cloudy day—it's a bonus if rain is predicted in the near future. If you don't have that flexibility, then plant in the early evening. Allow yourself more time than you think you'll need for planting. Water the new (or to be transplanted) plants the day before, or up to half an hour before planting.

2. Dig your hole into already amended or workable soil, no deeper than the pot or root ball of your plant, but twice as wide. Pile the excavated soil around the hole as you dig. Place a sprinkling of the removed soil—*not* compost, bark, or gravel—back into the bottom of the hole. If your soil needs those additions, they must be *thoroughly* mixed into a wider area than your planting hole so that there is uniformity in the soil. This is one case where the old practice of dumping compost in the bottom of a planting hole is just wrong.

3. Un-pot your plant and loosen the roots with your hands, working off most of the soil. If the un-potted plant appears to have its very own pot made of tangled roots, you'll need to cut into those. Slice along the sides and bottom with a knife. It sounds scary, but it is necessary or roots won't grow into their new home. Shrubs and trees can be grasped near the bottom of trunks, but most perennials need to be handled a bit more gently, so as not to snap stems.

4. Set the plant in the middle of the hole, spreading out roots. If the hole isn't big enough to accommodate the spread roots, dig it wider. Begin filling in with soil you removed, firming it in against the roots as you go. It is imperative that the roots make firm contact with their new soil.

5. Once all the soil is back in and tamped, make sure the level of the plant stem/root junction is not below the new soil level. If you're new at this, you will likely end up with that junction either too low or too high. No worries, just dig it out and try again. This is to be expected. Don't settle until the level is correct. In clay-based soils, it is better to err on the side of planting just a tad high rather than too deep. Sandy soils are so well aerated that planting a smidge deep is not a problem.

6. Once your plant is planted, finish firming it in with gentle foot pressure around all sides of the plant. If the soil sinks down significantly, add more, as long as that stem-root junction stays in the correct position. If the plant sustained any damage in the zeal of your labors, trim off broken twigs or stems. Otherwise, do not prune it. If the plant is small, mark it with tags in the ground so you can easily find them for the subsequent watering needed for your plant to become established.

7. Water the plant slowly and deeply to thoroughly soak the root zone. Water everything once, then go back and water again.

8. The last step is to top the area around the plant with mulch, just not too much: 2 inches for perennials, up to 4 inches for shrubs and trees, avoiding the area directly next to the trunks of woody plants or trees. You may water the mulch to settle it.

Some mulches resist water, and it's important over the next few weeks that consistent moisture get into the root zone. Pine needle straw allows a good flow of water, as does most newly spread hardwood hammered mulch. Pine bark mulches can repel water, but have good insulating and weed suppression properties. If you use pine bark mulch, disturb it with a rake before watering to allow good penetration. After watering, check underneath the mulch to be sure that water is soaking all the way through and getting to the roots below. Rock or chunks of plastic mulch aren't the best choices, as neither adds anything beneficial to the soil over time. We don't recommend landscape fabrics, as they can impede water and air flow.

Stand back and admire your work—such a good feeling! Care over the next few weeks consists of keeping moderate moisture in the root zone. As a general guide after spring planting, water by hand every three to five days (if no rain), for three weeks. After that, water once a week if there's been less than an inch of rain, for one minute per plant, throughout the summer (the 1-1-1 rule). Fall planting means less watering attention. Follow the 1-1-1 rule for one month. At this point, you may be thinking, "I thought native plants didn't require extra water!" Well, low to no supplemental water is in your future, but not until plants are well established, which means they've grown a significant root system in their new home.

As you look to that future, remember the traditional guideline about new plants: "The first year it sleeps, the second year it creeps, the third year it leaps." This is pretty much true in the Southeast, with its long growing season. Here, the winters of anticipation, the springs of over-activity, the summers of interminable heat, and the autumns of reflection have us always looking toward the next season and new beginnings.

Maintain

Maintenance is relative—what may be too much for one gardener is just getting started for another. The care it takes to keep a properly sited plant healthy is much less than what it takes to keep a bed edged, free of weeds, and perfectly pruned. The latter has nothing to do with whether a plant is native or not, it has to do with your visual preferences. Native plants have a lot to offer—habitat benefits, weathering climate extremes, wonderful variety, and a sense of place—but they won't satisfy traditional landscape aesthetics without maintenance. While it requires an investment, good hardscape (including hard edging) goes further to creating a neat and purposeful appearance in your garden

Natives such as orange coneflower (*Rudbeckia* 'Goldsturm') and switchgrass (*Panicum*) require limited maintenance when given optimal growing conditions, such as plenty of sun.

than anything else. And when done right, it is practically maintenance free.

If low maintenance is your number one priority, you'll need to front-load your labor and attention. In other words, choose plants carefully to match your soil and site, rather than experimenting with stretching them outside their preferences. Select woody plants that have natural shapes you like and whose ultimate sizes fit your space without needing to be pruned. Choose drought-tolerant perennials and grasses that are clumping, not creeping or fast spreading, and only require a once-a-year cutback. Pair these with amended soil, proper planting, and consistent watering during establishment, and you'll have little to do after that. Mulching once a year will cut down on weeds and buffer soil temperature and water retention. Supplemental water on established plants will only be needed in times of extreme drought.

The often-touted lower maintenance needs of natives may have as much to do with a change in viewpoint as the plants themselves. What pleases the eye often shifts when the narrow view of our landscapes as decoration expands into a 360-degree view of a functioning habitat. Seed heads become beautiful as bird feeders, twigs become architectural bee homes, and a stand of ornamental grasses in the winter becomes a sign of generosity, not neglect.

Health first

The most basic level of maintenance focuses on plant health. We may sound like a broken record, but many problems are avoided by "right plant, right place" and good plant establishment. However, native plants aren't immune to pests and diseases, especially invasive exotic insects and diseases.

If you notice problems like spots or insects on leaves, distorted growth, wilting even when the plant is well-watered, yellow foliage, or weird growths, the first step is to correctly identify what is causing the problem. The second step is to decide if it is truly a problem to the health of the plant or just a minor annoyance. It is often the latter. You'll probably start with an image search, app, or social media group, but if you're in doubt about your assessment, the extension service is a reliable resource. Besides online information, some extension offices allow samples to be sent to labs, others allow photographs to be submitted online. In either case, it's important to take a fairly large sample or an in-focus photograph both close-up and farther out. If you do identify a significant problem, listen to the advice given, but ask about the least-toxic options for addressing it.

Pests also come in larger packages with vigorous appetites. Deer, rabbits, and voles can wreak significant damage on plants under certain circumstances. If you're seeing more than a few of your plants disappear, take action. Research deterring strategies, then put some into action before these eaters make you want to throw in the trowel.

Weeds

Weeds are "pests" of the green persuasion. Generally not harmful to other plants, even if they compete for water and nutrients, weeds mostly offend us. With a common definition of "a plant growing out of place," there wouldn't be any weeds if we didn't have a "place" (garden) from which to expel them. Philosophy aside, weeds abide.

A plant might be considered a weed in one circumstance and not in another (a dandelion on the golf course versus a dandelion in your salad). However, we generally know a weed when we see it and there are seasonal patterns to their invasions. Some weeds are annuals, others perennials. Tree seedlings can be weeds, so can grass. If you are establishing a new bed or renovating an old one, it is imperative to dig out all perennial grass rhizomes, like Bermuda, as these can be near-impossible to fully eliminate when growing in and amongst your planting, rather than just creeping in from the edge.

The best way to weed is frequently. Weeding for twenty minutes once or twice a week is actually pleasant. Weeding for half a day once a month is not. By weeding more frequently, you'll prevent weeds from going to seed and eventually the number of seedlings will diminish. If possible, weed after a rain, when plants are much easier to pull. Weeds take advantage of space, especially bare ground. Your best defense against crops of weeds is mulch. And as garden plants get larger and ground covers cover ground, it will get harder for weeds to find a place to grow, reducing your work.

Beyond weeding

Mulching, adding compost, pruning a little, cutting back perennials, and watering as needed are the additional basics of maintaining the garden. The first four tasks are generally done once, at most twice, a year. Otherwise, a weekly walk through the garden to notice if plants have any major problems—severe wilting, yellowing, pests, or diseases—should be enjoyable. Address the negative surprises, but don't fail to enjoy the happy ones.

The prospect of pruning trees and shrubs can strike fear or fervor in gardeners. But other than removing dead or rubbing branches, pruning should be minimal if you have given your plants enough space, unless you desire a particular shape. Dead or damaged branches can be removed any time of year. Shrubs and trees bloom on either old growth from last year, or new twigs that they produce this year. If you prune the former before they bloom, you will be removing flower buds, so always plan to "prune soon after they bloom." A rule of thumb is to prune everything in late winter, *except* spring blooming species. There are a few tree species such as maple, birch, elm, and dogwood that "bleed sap" if pruned in late winter. These should be pruned in either summer or early winter.

Wild hydrangeas are well-suited throughout the Southeast; proper pruning will keep them at a manageable size.

Young trees may be pruned to remove crowded branches, but be sure you remove the entire branch or cut at a major junction. Do not "top" the main stem or cut a limb halfway back. Pruning large trees is the purview of an arborist and it's a good idea to have one take a look at your canopy trees every 5 to 7 years.

Some shrubs, but not all, require pruning as they mature. If you are pruning to shape or rejuvenate, there are two approaches. To make a shrub thicker with more but smaller blooms, you want to use a technique called heading back, where you prune off one-third or more of each twig. This will stimulate one or more new twigs to branch out and produce more flowers. On the other hand, if you have a dense, overgrown shrub that is not blooming well, you want to thin it out by removing older, whole stems to the ground. Remove a third of the total number each year and you will stimulate a new set of branches to grow each time you remove the oldest. These new branches will bloom vigorously for 2 to 3 years, then be ready to thin out and make way for new ones.

Natives with Low Deer Appeal

If you garden in an area where deer are forced to share habitat with humans, you will know it. Unless a 10-foot fence or an outdoor dog are in your budget, it's not possible to create an entirely deer-proof landscape. A deer will nibble any plant to try it, yet they do have preferences. Like a kid with a bucket of Halloween candy, some plants are immediately devoured, others are a last-resort. If you experience high deer pressure, consider the advice of native-garden designer Lisa Tompkins. "I use a training approach when adding new plants, by using some type of repellent, barricade, or motion-activated sprinkler from the beginning. Deer don't have a chance to get the idea that your garden is a feed lot. I place plants with high deer appeal closer to the house and those with low or no appeal toward the edges of properties." It is possible to share habitat without creating mortal enemies.

alumroot (*Heuchera*)

American wisteria (*Wisteria frutescens*)

beautyberry (*Callicarpa americana*)

black cohosh (*Actaea racemosa*)

bluestar (*Amsonia*)

common wild ginger (*Asarum canadense*)

cardinal flower (*Lobelia cardinalis*)

common wax-myrtle (*Morella cerifera*)

coral honeysuckle (*Lonicera sempervirens*)

eastern red cedar (*Juniperus virginiana*)

false indigo (*Baptisia*)

ferns (most; maidenhair an exception)

Florida anisetree (*Illicium floridanum*)

goldenrod (*Solidago*)

green-and-gold (*Chrysogonum virginianum*)

holly (*Ilex*)

Indian-pink (*Spigelia marilandica*)

mayapple (*Podophyllum peltatum*)

milkweed (*Asclepias*)

mint family perennials like bee-balm (*Monarda*), mountain mint (*Pycnanthemum*)

native palms (all species)

ornamental grasses (but not sedges)

pawpaw (*Asimina triloba*)

rattlesnake master (*Eryngium yuccifolium*)

red and bottlebrush buckeye (*Aesculus*)

spicebush (*Lindera benzoin*)

St. John's wort (*Hypericum*)

sweet-shrub (*Calycanthus floridus*)

yellow jessamine (*Gelsemium sempervirens*)

yucca (*Yucca*)

Ferns are not deer favorites, so they make a wise choice for garden borders.

Getting the Most from the Plant Profiles

The native plant profiles that follow are divided into seven chapters: Ferns, Grasses and Grasslike Plants, Woodland Wildflowers, Sun-Loving Perennials, Vines, Shrubs, and Trees. Each chapter begins with an introduction to the plant group, followed by individual native plant entries. Entry profiles are arranged in alphabetical order by Latin scientific name, which is the top name in each entry. Common names follow in large, bold type for easy searching. Profiles contain the following information about the plant:

- current scientific name (as well as any older scientific name, preceded by "syn.")
- common name
- typical habitat
- seasons of interest
- mature size (height × width)
- preferred light
- general description

In addition, symbols can be found to the right of the plant names to indicate which groups of wildlife—birds , hummingbirds , bees , butterflies , and/or caterpillars —directly benefit by using the plant as a food source.

Early native wildflowers like columbine attract important pollinators, such as this pipevine swallowtail butterfly.

Dig deeper

The last advice we have for you in utilizing this book is to extend it. When you find yourself wanting to know more, seek it out. Googling can be like opening a can of worms: there are some nice fat ones that are just what you need and a whole lot of tiny, wriggly ones that get in the way. We highly recommend getting to know the website and resources of your regional native plant society. Often they have lists of the plants most suitable to local environments. Likewise, your regional extension service website will have local gardening advice.

Wildflower.org has a searchable database of native plants that allows you to select desired plant characteristics to filter results. Xerces.org for pollinator gardens and Audubon.org for bird-friendly gardens are good starting points, as well. For cross-referenced information about native plants in the wild, namethatplant.net has a wealth of information, including plant identification, photographs, range maps, and Latin name pronunciations.

Ferns

Ferns are found in virtually every habitat in the Southeast. They are primitive plants that reproduce sexually not by seeds, but by microscopic spores which are produced in clusters called sori located on the undersides of the leaves. Their fine leaf texture can add an important element to your garden. Fern leaves are called fronds, and they develop by uncoiling from newly formed structures called fiddleheads.

It is important to know whether your fern is a "creeper" or a "clumper," for that will determine how it mixes with other plants. Creeping ferns can be as invasive as any fast-growing perennial; on the other hand, creepers can make useful ground covers in the right location. Clumpers can be planted throughout the shady perennial garden or grouped for aesthetic appeal. Sun lovers look great around pond gardens or in moist areas.

Most ferns are deciduous and their leaves die down in winter, but some are evergreen, which adds interest to the winter landscape. Most are not particularly drought tolerant and are shade loving, while others can tolerate sun if kept moist. Most prefer what we would call rich soil with ample organic matter for holding some moisture, but by no means do they require such regular watering as to keep them wet.

Adiantum capillus-veneris

southern maidenhair fern

moist woods, on limestone rocks and soil

spring, summer, fall

1 × 2 ft.

shade to part shade

This is a delicate, pretty fern that forms a loose ground cover in most soils. It also grows among limestone or acidic rocks and walls and may naturalize in rock walls. The irregularly shaped fronds have leaflets that are shaped like wedges and can form a handlike array of foliage. Southern maidenhair fern can be a specimen in a fernery, rockery, or woodland garden, and mixes well creeping among larger wildflowers and under open shrubs. It is easily thinned if it becomes too lavish, and is a great performer in all southern gardens through the warmer parts of hardiness zone 7.

Adiantum pedatum

northern maidenhair fern

rich woods throughout the Upper Southeast

spring, summer, fall

1.5 × 2–3 ft.

shade, part shade, morning sun

There is no more distinctive or lovely fern for Southeast gardens than maidenhair fern. Each deciduous frond displays a unique horseshoe-shaped arrangement of the leaflets (pinnae), which are held in a horizontal symmetrical circle. From the time the pinkish fiddleheads begin to unfurl and expand into frilly fronds, you will find this attractive plant a joy to behold. No garden should be without it. Use it as a bold specimen in spacious ferneries or rockeries, or mix it with larger wildflowers and small shrubs. Because it slowly spreads, it will eventually overtake nearby plants; but it is easy to thin out. Northern maidenhair fern withstands heat and drought fairly well, but once it wilts, there is no recovery and new fronds must regrow after watering.

Athyrium asplenioides

southern lady fern

rich and moist woods

spring, summer, fall

1–2 × 1–2 ft.

shade, part shade, morning sun

A deciduous clumper, southern lady fern is one of the most common ferns in the South, growing in moist woods and swamps. In the mountains, where the climate is cooler and wetter, it may form massive swaths along open, sunny road banks, where it will appear stiffly erect and a lighter green. In the shade, southern lady fern is open and more delicate and lacy—a typical-looking fern. The fronds, which often have characteristic red stipes (stalks) and are somewhat brittle, can be rejuvenated by carefully removing older and broken fronds, or cutting the fronds back altogether. It makes a bold landscape statement in woodland gardens and borders. Easy to grow in almost any situation and very reliable, southern lady fern is somewhat drought tolerant but will wilt when dry, only to perk up if watered soon.

Deparia acrostichoides*

silvery glade fern

moist forests

spring, summer, fall

1–2 × 1.5 ft.

shade, part shade, morning sun

This is a robust, erect, clumping fern. It is not massive, and mixes very well with wildflowers and other ferns, making it a favorite of many. The sturdy fronds are narrowly triangular and have a distinctive silvery gray cast. We like the way it stands out in a crowd as well as its highly touchable, finely fuzzy foliage. Silvery glade fern is somewhat drought tolerant and not fussy about soil. Because it is more upright, it may fit into tighter spots—and it might like a brighter spot than other ferns. This is one of the easiest ferns to grow.

*syn. Athyrium thelypterioides

Dryopteris ×australis

Dixie wood-fern

swamps

spring, summer, fall, semievergreen in winter

3–4 × 3–4 ft.

shade to morning sun

This massive, fast-growing, semievergreen clumper forms very robust, ever-enlarging patches over time. It is a natural hybrid between a northern and southern species, and must be given room to spread in exercising its hybrid vigor. The colonies may be thinned by removal (division) of growths around the edges. It loves moisture, but is quite tolerant of drought and some sun. While neatly standing at ordered attention all summer, by winter, the huge, thick fronds will come to lie conspicuously on the ground—forming a noticeable ground covering. By spring, the vigorous fiddleheads, covered with brushy brown scales, come up as a rising army. It may be confused with either of its parents, both of which make good, large garden plants. The northern log fern (*Dryopteris celsa*) is deciduous, shorter with a little wider frond; the southern wood-fern (*D. ludoviciana*) is tough and fully evergreen, with a narrower and very shiny frond. Neither is as robust as its hybrid offspring.

sori clusters of Dixie wood-fern

Dryopteris marginalis

marginal wood-fern

rich woods, often on rocks, in the Upper Southeast

spring, summer, fall, winter

1.5 × 1.5 ft.

shade to part shade

Marginal wood-fern is an evergreen clumper growing from a single crown, forming a symmetrical, open funnel shape—much like a large badminton birdie. It is very attractive and formal in its growth habit, staying put as a single growth (or tight clump). A bit fussy about moisture as it does not want to be too dry, it must also be well drained, a situation difficult to create in the warmer parts of the Southeast. Its distinctive dark green leathery leaves are not highly dissected. Somewhat similar is the large and stately Goldie's fern (*Dryopteris goldiana*), with a broader, more robust frond exhibiting a light greenish sheen. It is more northerly, coming southward only in the mountains, where it is cooler and wetter and therefore not as suitable south of zone 7. Similarly, fancy fern (*D. intermedia*) can be used in the more northern zones and in the mountains as a fine-textured and striking evergreen fern specimen.

*Matteuccia struthiopteris**

ostrich fern

moist-wet woods

spring, summer, fall, winter

2–4 × 2–4 ft.

shade, part shade, morning sun

A remarkable giant (up to 5 ft. tall or more in the wild), ostrich fern is found in the wet woodlands of the Northeast, barely reaching Virginia. Its formal clumps look like giant shuttlecocks, and each crown vigorously sends out 3–7 long underground runners that result in extensive colonies. So—plant an ostrich fern, then jump back! The young fiddleheads are a choice edible delicacy. The maturing fronds are beautiful and deciduous, but the separate, brown, 2 ft. tall, spore-bearing fronds become hardened and persist through the winter, making them an outstanding landscape feature. Keep it under control by digging the unwanted runner offsets in the spring. The traditional ostrich fern is not heat tolerant and will not persist south of zone 6. Now, however, heat-tolerant strains are available, and *must be* utilized in the Southeast. Two such heat-proof cultivars are 'The King' and 'Fanfare'.

*syn. *M. pensylvanica*

Onoclea sensibilis

sensitive fern

marshes and swamps

spring, summer, fall, winter

1–2 × 1–2 ft.

shade to part sun

A deciduous creeper with widely spaced fronds on long-running rhizomes that form dense colonies, sensitive fern grows quickly, making a coarse-textured mass. While stately, this fern should not be used with other plants. It could have a place in a very moist or wet situation around a pond, under tall shrubs in a wetland, or in other isolated situations. It is very sensitive to drought and cold, and new fronds are often killed by late frosts—hence the common name. A few strange-looking, spore-bearing fronds are produced in late summer with leaf tissues formed into round, beadlike structures harboring sori, brown and firm in texture, persisting through the winter. Sensitive fern can be distinguished from the similar netted chain fern (*Woodwardia areolata*) by sensitive fern's smooth-edged frond-lobes that are opposite each other, plus its tough, persistent, fertile fronds. Netted chain fern has minutely toothed margins, alternate lobes, and fertile fronds that wither in winter.

Osmunda spectabilis*

royal fern

moist woods and wet situations

spring, summer, fall

1.5–5 × 2–4 ft.

part shade to part sun

Royal fern goes hand in hand with cinnamon fern as a striking deciduous clumper. Its large and stiffly erect-to-spreading fronds arise via attractive fiddleheads, often forming dense masses of tough black roots around each crown. If you want a big, easy fern, this is it! The coarse-textured fronds are a delight to watch unfurl; the terminal pinnae are replaced by clusters of brownish, globular, spore-bearing tissue that withers by summer. It seems to adapt to any situation, but is especially good in moist-to-wet areas and in bright shade to mostly sun (with supplemental watering). It can become overwhelming in size when grown well. If kept on the dry and shady side, royal fern will remain small, providing the coarse texture for which it is renowned, and still have good fall color. The more sun and moisture it receives, the larger it grows.

*syn. O. regalis

Osmundastrum cinnamomeum*

cinnamon fern

rich woods and wet situations

spring, summer, fall

2–5 × 1–2 ft.

part shade to part sun

Well known, large, and gorgeous, cinnamon fern makes a prominent and stately specimen. It is suitable for almost any location in a rich woodland fernery or around ponds and moist planting areas. It is a deciduous clumper, with very large and stiffly erect fronds from a crown of tough, wiry roots, often forming open colonies. The unfurling hair-covered fiddleheads are as attractive as they come, and the variable textures add much interest. In spring, individual spore-bearing fronds arise bearing a thick, millet-like plume of cinnamon-brown tissue that soon withers. In autumn, the fronds turn a striking bronze-yellow that rivals any other fall color. The tough root mass is nearly impossible to divide without a root saw. It can crowd out smaller plants, so watch spacing. Exposure to persistently dry soil will cause it to grow smaller and smaller. Plants in full sun must be kept moist for best results; you cannot overwater it unless you permanently submerge it.

*syn. *O. cinnamomea*

Phegopteris hexagonoptera*

broad beech fern

rich wooded slopes

spring, summer, fall

1 × 1.5 ft.

shade to part shade

Broad beech fern is a deciduous creeper, forming large, dense colonies from long, shallow rhizomes. It is beautiful to behold because of the architectural structure of its almost perfectly triangular leaves, which have many lobes instead of complete segment divisions. Give it room to spread, however, and the more you water it, the larger it will grow and the faster it will colonize. Do not plant with delicate spring wildflowers, but we love it among shrubs and larger perennials and even along paths where you can walk through several planted together. It is easily transplanted or thinned out and is tolerant of heat but not drought. The fronds are brittle, but regrow readily.

*syn. Thelypteris hexagonoptera

Polystichum acrostichoides

Christmas fern

moist deciduous forests

spring, summer, fall, winter

1.5 × 1.5 ft.

shade to part shade

This is a robust, clump-forming fern with fronds that are not as divided as other ferns—hence offering a slightly coarser texture. Easily recognized, it is a lovely and durable fern, easily divided and transplanted. It can provide path edging, background, and a good companion for many woodland wildflowers and shrubs. Christmas fern is an excellent evergreen specimen for winter appeal in the fernery or woodland glen. It should be in every garden, and can grow in a variety of moisture-holding, humus-rich soils. This tough, dark green fern is tolerant of morning sun, moist to dryish conditions, and heat and cold. One of the favorite stories to help children recognize Christmas fern is to hold a single leaflet vertically to resemble a Christmas stocking with heel and toe (the enlarged basal lobe).

Christmas fern fiddleheads

Thelypteris kunthii

southern shield fern

swamps and low woods

spring, summer, fall

1–2 × 1–2 ft.

part shade to part sun

Southern shield fern has taken the gardening world by storm in the last three decades. It is wonderfully robust and graceful, forming dense, gray-green masses in light shade or morning sun (if kept moist). It is a deciduous (or semievergreen southward) creeper that creates very dense, fast-growing colonies. This is a striking plant for borders, backgrounds, path enclosures, or patches with larger shrubs in the non-mountainous Southeast. It is aggressive—adaptable and drought tolerant, even volunteering readily from spores in normal garden situations. Do not overwater and it will be less aggressive. Be careful to not plant southern shield fern with other plants, as it will choke them out. However, it is very worthwhile in the right location, all by itself with room to grow. Try it where nothing else will grow. This is a landscaper's space-filling dream for ease and beauty.

Thelypteris noveboracensis

New York fern

dryish woods

spring, summer, fall

1 × 1 ft.

shade to part sun

This fern can make a graceful, fast-growing deciduous ground cover. Because it is not tough, just relentless, it may blend well with other sturdy woodland plants, but we like to keep the New York fern away from most small wildflowers. In nature, it can form extensive colonies, filling up the woods with an endless sea of delicate green, especially in shady situations where other plants will not grow. We have seen no other fern (or plant for that matter) capable of carpeting the mountain woodlands so uniformly. While delicately spreading, it is easily thinned out and transplanted. It may not be so heat tolerant in the Deep South, so provide extra water during the hottest weather. New York fern has brittle fronds that regrow readily if broken. The lower leaflets (pinnae) reduce in size gradually down the stalk, making it distinctive among creeping ferns.

Grasses and Grasslike Plants

Here in the Southeast, we have distinctive native grass species in every habitat—from the shifting sand dunes of the coast to the stormy tops of the highest mountains; from wettest to driest, and in every form; from bold and striking to diminutive and obscure. Grasses have taken their place in the ornamental garden by virtue of their sparse water needs and their outstanding textural manifestations. These contrasting forms and colors work well with other perennials and may last well into the winter months, when dried grasses are a subtle, scratchy string quartet (or percussion rhythm section) in the background mood of the garden. As for maintenance, grasses are best planted in spring as the weather warms. And in later winter, before new growth starts, be sure to cut them back. Small birds will forage on the seedheads of many grasses through the winter.

Andropogon gerardii

big bluestem

meadows, roadsides, and open woods

summer, fall, winter

5–8 × 1 ft.

full sun

The tallest of the desirable, ornamental native grasses, this elegant plant is unmistakable with its tight, upright, green to blue-green, leafy clumps topped by three-clustered flower spikes in late summer. Slow to start growth in spring but easy to grow in lean, dryish soil, big bluestem does not like overwatering or a site in shade. In such conditions it becomes lush and tends to flop over. Planted as individuals or in masses, it offers an element of stateliness to the meadow garden or sunny perennial border. The cultivar 'Red October' has distinctive red-purple stems in the fall. Big bluestem can be quite dramatic, especially in autumn and winter, when the rustle of the dried stems stimulates our sense of sound like no other garden plant.

Andropogon ternarius

split-beard bluestem

meadows and roadsides

summer, fall, winter

1–2 × 1–2 ft.

full sun

Split-beard bluestem is a smaller, less robust, and more clumping plant than big bluestem, with purplish leaves and very attractive, white, fluffy seed heads in autumn. These charming little feathery plumes are fabulous for their up-close details and are used as cut stems. As with most southern grasses, planting is best in the warm spring. It becomes showy in late summer. Split-beard bluestem is easy to grow in well-drained soils and should be more widely used as it fits in well with other kinds of perennials in the border, bed, or meadow. It holds its color well into winter. Other commonly seen bluestem grasses include broom-straw (*Andropogon virginicus*), aka broom-sedge, and brushy-bluestem (*A. glomeratus*). These species are the conspicuous grasses seen abundantly across the region in old fields and roadside embankments. While striking, they will seed themselves aggressively around the garden and so are best enjoyed in the wild.

Carex laxiculmis

creeping sedge

rich woods

spring, summer, fall, winter

1 × 1 ft.

part shade to shade

Creeping sedge does not really creep very fast, but makes attractive clumps of loose, arching foliage with ½-inch-wide blades and can grow in shade or part sun if kept moist. The bluish foliage is attractive in formal and informal settings, especially in poorer woodland soils where other plants may not thrive, and may be planted densely as a ground cover. It works well with woodland wildflowers and holds its leaves all year round. There is a beautiful blue-leaved form trademarked as Bunny Blue™. A very similar species, blue wood sedge (*Carex flacco-sperma*), forms an attractive, 1 × 1 ft., clumping to slowly spreading mound for the shade garden, and may tolerate drier conditions.

Carex pensylvanica

Pennsylvania sedge

dryish woods

spring, summer, fall

6 × 6 in.

part sun to shade

This clumping sedge has soft, narrow leaves and forms tufts with a delicate, wispy appearance. It makes a fine-textured ground cover in dryish conditions and dappled shade or part sun, where grasses are not happy. Not aggressive, it may be used around woodland wildflowers and shrubs and to fill in bare spots. It is quite cold hardy, but may not like the heat of the Deep South. The slowly spreading clumps always look a bit disheveled. As an effective no-mow lawn substitute, it can be mowed in late winter to keep it neat. Two very similar species are the Appalachian sedge (*Carex appalachica*) and Texas sedge (*C. texensis*). Both of these species are good lawn alternatives under large trees and in woodland gardens. They may perform better in warmer regions, and may be evergreen farther south.

Carex plantaginea

seersucker sedge

rich woods

spring, summer, winter, fall

1.5 × 1.5 ft.

part shade to shade

This wonderful sedge was one of the first wild species to adorn Larry's shady wildflower garden 40 years ago. It is reliably evergreen, forming loose clumps with grass-green, ribbon-like leaves to 1 in. wide, distinctively crinkled and becoming gracefully lax. The small spring flowers are worth noticing on tall, graceful stems, but are not what you'd call showy. It's not fussy about soil, mixes well with all kinds of herbaceous plants and ferns, and looks soothing on gentle slopes and ledges in a woodland setting. Suitable as a ground cover or in groupings, seersucker sedge is long lived. If sufficiently moist, it will naturalize readily, but it is not aggressive. This is a first-rate companion plant for any woodland setting.

Chasmanthium latifolium*

river-oats

moist woods and creek banks

summer, fall

2–3 × 1–2 ft.

sun to shade

This is a widely known and attractive grass, forming strongly upright clumps and producing conspicuous, ¾ in. long, flattened spikelets on dangling stalks. The whole plant is attractively more lax in shade, dried stems often lasting through the winter. It can be especially handsome for informal woodlands and shaded settings, and more formal in borders, groupings, path edgings, and containers. Seedlings readily self-sow, but are easily removed. River-oats was a very popular garden plant decades ago, but has fallen somewhat out of favor, perhaps because they seed aggressively and everybody has one. If this is your first encounter, you can solve these problems by obtaining one from a friend as a pass-along-plant and by practicing responsible "plant parenting" by deadheading (cutting off) the old seed heads after they are enjoyed, but before they start shedding seeds. In the fall, it is tinged pink and gold.

*syn. Uniola latifolia

Eragrostis elliottii 'Wind Dancer'

Elliott's love grass

roadsides, meadows, woods

summer, fall, winter

2–3 × 2–3 ft.

sun

'Wind Dancer' love grass is the best cultivar of this species. The blue-green foliage makes a fine-textured mound, from which ascend numerous 3 to 4 ft. tall, cloudlike clusters of tiny flowers/fruit. These move in the breeze and add a unique structural form to the garden. Grow this grass as a mass in the border, as a background, on a steep bank as erosion control, or in an area that is difficult to mow. While drought toler-ant, it appreciates lean, moist soil. You will love the protrusive puffs of palliative plumes in late summer that last well into fall and winter. Other cultivars, such as 'Tallahassee Sunset' (which is half as tall as 'Wind Dancer') and other species, such as purple love grass (*Eragrostis spectabilis*) are adaptable throughout the Southeast.

![Elliott's love grass plant in a garden setting with feathery blue-green foliage and ferns behind]

Muhlenbergia capillaris

pink muhly

savannas and woods

summer, fall, winter

3–4 × 3–4 ft.

sun

Pink muhly is an absolute showstopper, one of the most distinctive grasses for fall color. The effect is a dense cloud of pink spray. It is informal and clump forming, with narrow leaves and enormous plumes of tiny pink flowers September to November, lasting dried into winter. It is especially useful in masses in difficult places such as road banks, traffic medians, and "hell strips" (that forlorn area between the sidewalk and the street), enduring dry or sandy soils and tolerating salt spray at the coast. Use pink muhly also as ground cover or accent in large borders and beds, as well as near water features and foundations. Another big plus—as with most grasses—it is not favored by deer. It also comes as a white muhly.

Panicum virgatum

switch grass

meadows, marshes, pinelands

summer, fall, winter

2–8 × 2–3 ft.

sun

In the wild, switch grass is large and informal, distinctive in producing tall, multibranched clouds of flower stalks. There are more than 12 named cultivars that emphasize various features, including stiffly upright growth and steel-blue foliage ('Heavy Metal'), more lax and broadly billowing greenish growth ('Hänse Herms'), bluish green foliage ('Cloud Nine'), columnar habit ('Northwind'), and informal red foliage ('Shenandoah'), all of which can be used in rain gardens. The clumps are variously shaped and may slowly spread. Flowering in mid- to late summer, they produce attractive plumes of tiny flowers that become impressive rustling hay sheaves in winter. While tolerant of a variety of soils and moisture levels, it is best grown in average to lean soil in full sun. Switch grass can be planted in borders and beds, as specimens, as screening, or as a line of demarcation.

*Schizachyrium scoparium**

little bluestem grass

meadows, roadsides, and woods

summer, fall, winter

3–4 × 2–4 ft.

sun

Along with big bluestem and Indian grass, little bluestem is a hallmark of the original American prairies. Several cultivars have better bluish stems (for example, 'The Blues'). It is strictly clump forming, with leaves green to bluish, turning orangish to reddish in fall and into winter. Flowers appear in late summer, producing delicate, silvery tufts of plumage along the drying stems. This is a garden grass that works well as a specimen in its own right, is truly exceptional in mass plantings, mixes well with other plants in the border, and may even work in rain gardens, as it is tolerant of various soils and moisture. Use in full sun.

*syn. *Andropogon scoparius*

Sorghastrum nutans

Indian grass

meadows, roadsides, woods

summer, fall, winter

3–7 × 1–2 ft.

sun

This is our favorite big grass, elegantly robust in form but delicate in flower. It is strictly clump forming to 7 ft. tall, with leaves that are green to bluish, then turn yellow to orange in autumn and persist into winter. It is perhaps the showiest of the grasses, thanks to its conspicuous yellow floral stamens in late summer to early autumn. Along with the bluestems, this is a characteristic species of the American tallgrass prairie. Walking among the roadside clumps of Indian grass today, it's easy to imagine how majestic the mature prairies must have been in their heyday. We're glad we have this representative so common in the Southeast. Indian grass has the beautiful blue-stemmed (and leaved) cultivars 'Sioux Blue' and 'Indian Steel'.

Stenotaphrum secundatum

St. Augustine grass

edges of coastal brackish marshes

spring, summer, fall, winter

4–8 in., vigorously creeping

sun to part sun

Walk on it, play on it, scratch your naked back on it. Here's your only choice for a native lawn grass if you live in the Mid- to Deep South, and it rarely needs mowing (or fertilizing). It is somewhat evergreen and spreads vigorously from creeping stems forming a dense, neat ground cover in sandy or loamy soil, in sun or very light shade. It may reach 6–8 in. tall if well watered, and will choke out virtually all common summer weeds. The leaves are green, 4 in. long and ⅜ in. wide. Late summer flowers are inconspicuous on short, uniquely flattened spikes. Great for lawns and informal ground cover—you can start it from rooted runners pulled up from another lawn, or you can buy it as sod. It has a much coarser texture than any other southern lawn grass, and is drought tolerant. It turns tan in winter. Because it spreads, it must be trimmed periodically along flower beds, driveways, and paths, but this is not unlike several other lawn grasses (and this one does not burrow underground like Bermuda grass). Grown for years throughout the coastal South, it is becoming more widely planted as winters become milder (it is not happy prolonged below 15°F).

Woodland Wildflowers

Woodland wildflowers are those that come up in spring in the understory of the forest canopy. They are a sight to behold as winter turns into spring, and the first trout lilies and bloodroot poke their heads above the leaf litter. Then one day they all burst into bloom, reaching a crescendo as dozens more come along by midspring.

The secret behind the suddenness of their appearance is the fact that they must come up and bloom, set seed, and store food in underground roots, tubers, and bulbs for next year—all before the forest canopy leafs out and strong sunlight disappears. So the competitive rush to attract pollinators commands each species to display its disproportionately large and showy flowers for the bees and butterflies, seemingly all at once.

Planting a wildflower garden is simple: you need some shade, woodland soil (rich in organic matter) and a collection of species to get started. Plant them in groupings of threes (at least) to allow them to cross-pollinate and make more seeds to proliferate their numbers.

Actaea pachypoda

doll's-eyes

rich woods

spring, fall

1–2 × 1–2 ft.

part shade to part sun

Doll's-eyes is a clumping perennial with multidivided leaves. The short-lived, fluffy white spring flowers are moderately showy and the foliage looks good all summer, but its main value is in the striking white berries (which are readily eaten by birds) that appear on thick red stalks. It is worth the wait for these berries to mature. This is a good plant for the woodland garden, but note that that it has only a brief sparkle in spring and then—wow!—the notable white fruit in late summer. Cultivar 'Misty Blue' has attractive bluish green foliage.

doll's-eyes flower

doll's-eyes fruit

Actaea racemosa*

black cohosh

dryish woods
early summer
3–6 × 2–4 ft.
part shade to part sun

Black cohosh is a stunning garden plant, coming into bloom after most other spring flowers are past their prime, giving a wonderful boost to the open shade garden. Native bees love the spikes of fluffy, white bottlebrush flowers. It provides bold architectural form with its very broad (to 3+ ft.) divided leaves and tall, flowering stalks that feature small dried pods after blooms have faded. Specimens slowly but surely spread to form large patches, which make wonderful scenes in the garden, so give them room. The tough, knotty rhizomes can easily be divided in early spring to thin the colony.

*syn. Cimicifuga racemosa

Aquilegia canadensis

eastern columbine

woods and rock outcrops

spring

2–3 × 1–2 ft.

part shade to part sun

Eastern columbine, a classic favorite for people and early hummingbirds, is among the first spring wildflowers to bloom and continues through late spring. Its pendulous red and yellow flowers are cheerful and fascinating, and we would not be without them throughout the garden. Plants are short-lived evergreen perennials persisting for 1–2 years. It self-sows readily in most soils, so you will always have a few around. Let them grow where they will; they're easily removed where not wanted. The one drawback of eastern columbine is its susceptibility to disfiguring leaf miners and powdery mildew. Remove infected leaflets early to reduce future damage. Several charming dwarf selections, to about 8 in. tall, closely resemble the species: 'Canyon Vista', 'Little Lanterns', and 'Nana'.

Arisaema triphyllum

common Jack-in-the-pulpit

moist forests and bottomlands

spring, summer, fall

1–2 × 1–2 ft.

part shade to shade

Jack-in-the-pulpit is a common and well-known wildflower, found in almost every woodland near a creek. There, they form colonies from underground tubers (which are not edible). Some folks confuse it with a pitcher plant or lady's slipper orchid, but Jack-in-the-pulpit's distinct flowering structure has a hood designed to keep out rainwater and surround the spikes of tiny male or female flowers. You will need plants of both sexes nearby to get the delightful clusters of red berries in late fall—so plant several specimens together. Some plants are entirely green; others develop hoods with deep purple and white stripes. Younger plants may die down in dry summers, but don't worry, they'll be back. Every woodland garden should have a Jack somewhere, at least for the kids to see and wonder, *What is that?*

Asarum canadense

common wild ginger

rich woods and bottomlands

spring, summer, fall

6 in. × 1 ft., spreading

shade to part shade

Often called Canada ginger, this attractive, dense ground cover produces kidney-shaped leaves with a soft texture. It covers well, growing over and around anything in its way. In that sense, it is too aggressive for associating with delicate wildflowers. And it is not evergreen, leaving the ground bare in winter. Nevertheless, it is a pleasing sight and very easy to grow. It readily makes seeds, and you will have little satellite colonies popping up everywhere as the seeds are dispersed by ants. Fortunately, the seedlings are easy to dig and remove. The broken stems smell of ginger, but it is not readily edible. The creeping stems can choke out weeds and other wildflowers.

Asarum harperi

'Callaway' ginger

bogs and streambanks

spring, summer, fall, winter

1–2 in. × 1–2 ft., slowly spreading

shade to part shade

'Callaway' ginger is a rare form of heartleaf ginger (*Asarum* or *Hexastylis shuttleworthii*) from central Alabama, vigorous in cultivation and widely grown. While all heart-leaf gingers are evergreen, this species is stoloniferous and creeps to eventually cover a large area. The specific selection 'Callaway' is exceptional, with tight, small, dark green leaves and silver mottling. It is great in the garden and attracts lots of attention. It likes moist, well-drained acidic soil, taking a few years to become established and begin forming its magical carpet. The flowers are sparsely produced little brown jugs held under the leaves. Get a plant, find a suitable spot, and be patient!

Cardamine concatenata*

cutleaf toothwort

rich woods

spring

6 × 6 in.

shade to dappled shade

We love this species of cutleaf toothwort because it comes up early in the woodland wildflower garden along with the trilliums, slowly spreading from underground tubers without overpowering. It offers profuse narrow foliage and numerous ½ in. wide, long-lasting, pinkish white flowers—all in just the right proportions to provide a fill-in with other wildflowers. By the end of spring it has died down for the rest of the year—but next spring it will multiply. Its well-known relative, common toothwort (*Cardamine diphylla*), is an excellent wintergreen ground cover with shiny, dark green, waxy, thick leaves, producing many white flowers in spring. Plant enough so it fills in quickly. Note that these species go dormant in summer, so surround them with other delicate, non-spreading wildflowers, like bloodroot, windflower, or ferns, which can take over as the toothworts go to sleep.

*syn. C. laciniata

Chrysogonum virginianum

green-and-gold

woods

spring, summer, fall, winter

3–6 in. × 3–6 in., spreading

shade to part shade

A gem of a garden plant, green-and-gold spreads as a low evergreen ground cover, with just the right aggressiveness to mix with other sturdy wildflowers in a shady garden. It holds through hot, cold, and dry conditions. In a bit more sun, it may form a denser mat. After the plant's profuse yellow spring bloom, you will probably find at least one flower in your colony nearly any day of the growing season. While tolerant of many soil types, it does not like to be overwatered. We are very fond of this species in all seasons and would encourage you to find a place for it in your garden, especially on banks or open areas between other plants. There are several selections, including 'Allen Bush', a more clump-forming cultivar, and 'Norman Singer', a spreading selection that grows a compact mat.

Dicentra eximia

bleeding-heart

rich woods

spring, summer

1 × 1 ft.

part shade to part sun

Bleeding-heart is the cutest wildflower, evoking wonder and curiosity as to how the strange heart-shaped flower is put together. It is a short-lived (1–2 years) perennial from brittle roots, forming a mound of incredibly delicate, fern-like leaves from which arise stalked clusters of pendulous pink flowers. Bleeding-heart can brighten a woodland garden, especially as it keeps blooming even after the rush of spring is over. With supplemental watering, it can bloom all summer, even in very hot weather. Seedlings can come up in many different places to keep your garden supplied. There are several robust and attractive selections, even white ones, mostly derived from hybrids with Pacific bleeding-heart (*Dicentra formosa*). However, while many of these cultivars are suitable, we find the straight species performs better in the warm Southeast.

Erigeron pulchellus

robin's-plantain

woods and meadow margins

spring, summer, fall

1 ft., spreading

part sun to part shade

Robin's-plantain is a choice plant all by itself, creating a dense colony of large leaves that hug the ground like a disheveled throw rug. The leafy rosettes touch as the patch spreads by sending out new runners. It loves road banks and edges and is often found along trails, on rocky slopes, even on flat ground where it will not be covered by heavy leaf mulch. The early spring flowers are daisylike and soft pink with yellow centers; heads are 1 to 1½ in. wide, clustered atop mostly leafless stems. A patch of them all blooming at once is attractive—and fragrant, too.

Erythronium umbilicatum

dimpled trout lily

rich woods and bottomlands

early spring

6 in., spreading

shade to part sun

Trout lily is a well known and charming wildflower that produces lovely yellow flowers in late winter—often the first wildflower to emerge and bloom—and eventually forms a solid ground cover, with its characteristic speckled leaves. Use trout lilies as patches and masses in the garden, especially on little hillsides and with evergreen Christmas ferns. The flowers are shy and hang down, except in bright sun. It is a mystery why it does not always bloom profusely given that there are so many plants in one place, each leaf growing from a very deep bulb. The flower forms a single round seed pod that lies on the ground, with an indentation on the end. The leaves are gone before spring is over, but they are something to look forward to each year as winter's tedium wears on and we ask, "Are the trout lilies blooming yet?"

Eurybia divaricata*

white wood aster

dryish woods

summer, fall, winter

1.5 ft., spreading

part shade to part sun

White wood aster is a beautiful late-summer plant, even though it is not as colorful as some of its sun-loving relatives. The showy, 1 in. wide flowers are reminiscent of daisies, white with a yellow center, produced in broad, flat-topped clusters atop black zigzag stems, blooming late summer into autumn. It spreads tenaciously in any soil, and is wonderful on dry, rocky slopes or difficult situations where you can't (or don't want to) grow anything else. The leaves are attractive in themselves, with a minimal winter presence. You cannot manage it by pulling it up (the stems break off), so watch where you plant it. The more you cut it back, the more it grows back and blooms, especially in shade. The cultivars 'Eastern Star', 'Raiche', and 'Silver Star' are excellent, with clean white flowers that are a bit shorter.

*syn. Aster divaricatus

Geranium maculatum

wild geranium

rich woods

spring

1.5 × 1.5 ft.

part shade to part sun

Easy to grow, wild geranium produces numerous cheerful, 1 in. wide, pink-blue flowers in springtime. Its fruit is quick to mature into thin, pointy pods that are fun for kids: the mature seeds separate at the base, then coil up like a spring and are flung off in dispersal, popping up as new plants later. This tough plant produces dark green, deeply cut leaves that add texture before they die down for the summer, making room for summer ferns. The clumps enlarge slowly, but are easy to thin out and divide. The cultivar 'Espresso' is more compact.

Heuchera americana

American alumroot

rock outcrops and dryish woods

spring, summer, fall, winter

1 × 2 ft.

part shade to part sun

American alumroot is one of our toughest wildflowers, with beautiful evergreen leaves that are scalloped and mottled with greens and pinks. It has staying power on well-drained sites; Larry has had one neglected clump for over 30 years, watered only during droughts. The plants can tolerate strong sunlight and well-drained soil once established, but giving extra water and too much fertilizer will shorten their life spans. The many new, beautiful *Heuchera* hybrids rarely last more than a year or two in the warm Southeast. The only selection we have found with staying power and beautiful leaves like specimens in the wild is 'Dale's Strain'. Others we like are yellow-leaved 'Citronelle' and yellow-with-reddish-blotches 'Tiramisu'. Other cultivars may do better in the cooler mountains. Giant alumroot (*H. macrorhiza*) cultivar 'Autumn Bride' has large, fuzzy leaves and can look great, but may become untidy in the summer heat. It perks up in fall and may be better in cooler regions.

Impatiens capensis

orange jewelweed

rich woods and mountain roadsides

summer, fall

2–4 × 1–2 ft.

shade to part sun

Jewelweed is one of the few native annuals grown in gardens. It is a fast-growing opportunist in the shade garden, and can become quite abundant from its annual seed crop—downright lush if the soil is kept moist. Among its soft green leaves, it produces charming orange flowers all summer, where bees and hummingbirds often encounter each other. We would be reluctant to recommend such an aggressive plant, except for its popularity with pollinators and the fun that happens when the ripe, turgid, little green seed pods are pinched and suddenly split open in a tiny explosion! They are easy to remove as seedlings, and I'd rather have a few too many than none at all. They keep blooming until the last hummingbird flies south. But be warned of their profusion.

Iris cristata

dwarf crested iris

rich woods

spring, summer

3–6 in. tall, spreading

shade to part sun

This native is a true charmer, spreading from a short-creeping, shallow rhizome to form a large colony. The plants brighten the spring woodland garden for a brief time with their showy blue and yellow flowers, then they sort of lay back and just vegetate until they die down for the winter. Spread them around and let them be understory ground cover for taller shrubs and ferns. Several selections are available: 'Eco Bluebird' is more vigorous, with darker flowers; 'Powder Blue Giant' is very vigorous and noticeably larger; 'Tennessee White' is a pure albino.

Maianthemum racemosum*

Solomon's-plume

rich woods

spring, summer, fall

1–2 × 1–2 ft.

shade to part sun

On wildflower-viewing field trips, we always have to differentiate between "true" Solomon's-seal (*Polygonatum biflorum*) and "false" Solomon's-seal or, as it's been more recently dubbed, Solomon's-plume. It forms informal clumps in the garden, providing a somewhat unusual growth pattern with its zigzaggy leaf arrangement. The very tiny white flowers in tip-of-the-stem plumes (versus the larger bell-shaped flowers that hang under the leaves of true Solomon's-seal) provide a special but brief show in spring and are displayed conspicuously. They are followed by a unique array of long-lasting, small, speckled red berries in late summer. Few other woodland wildflowers are as pretty in fruit.

*syn. Smilacina racemosa

fruit of Solomon's-plume

Mertensia virginica

Virginia bluebells

low woods

spring

1.5 × 1–2 ft.

shade to part shade

One of our all-time favorites, Virginia bluebells emerges very early and shows pink flower bud color as the floppy eared leaves stretch out. The 1½ in. wide flowers open blue, and the cluster of blooms and the stance of the vigorous clumps are very appealing. But this wildflower plays a surprising disappearing trick for a plant its size: the whole thing dies down completely in just a few weeks. We advise having other plants nearby to take its place. Mix Virginia bluebells with modest-sized deciduous ferns (for example, silvery glade or lady fern), or other late wildflowers such as Jack-in-the-pulpit, Jacob's-ladder, bleeding-heart, sweet Betsy trillium, or Indian-pink. We still wouldn't be without this adaptable and long-lived perennial. Its early absence makes the heart grow fonder, but don't worry; it will be back next spring.

Mitchella repens

partridge-berry

dryish woods

spring, summer, fall, winter

1–2 in., spreading

shade to part sun

This wonderful plant has a paradoxical character. It has been called a subshrub with minute woody stem growth, but gets only 1 in. tall. It forms an evergreen, mat-forming colony from a creeping stem on top of the ground. The twin white flowers appear in late spring from most pairs of leaves—another prize to send the kids out to hunt, because the plants are so close to the ground. We have seen it in dry acid soil under hemlock trees, and in moist floodplains. Larry has some plants forming a small mat in full sun in loamy soil—partridge-berry does not like full sun, but it survives. Male and female flowers are on separate plants, and you will need both growing together to get the charming little bright red berries that are conspicuous all winter—unless the partridges get to them first.

Pachysandra procumbens

Allegheny-spurge

rich woods

spring, summer, fall, winter

6 in. × 1 ft., spreads

shade to part shade

Allegheny-spurge is our most attractive evergreen ground cover and has a wonderful presence, forming colonies from creeping rhizomes. The ovate leaves are an olive green, typically with silver mottling, bronzing in winter sun; they always seem to look great. The small, less conspicuous white flower clusters are interesting but often overlooked in March. Because it chokes out other plants, it cannot be used in close combinations with other wildflowers, though we have seen trilliums come up in the middle of a patch. It is heat and drought tolerant, and can take flooding. It can grow in dense shade, is especially good on uneven or rocky sites, and can be removed from the edges to keep the mass confined. Plant or transplant in late winter or spring, not fall. A cultivar with consistently good silver markings is 'Silver Streak'.

Packera aurea*

golden ragwort

moist woods and bottomlands

spring, summer, winter

2 × 1 ft., spreading

part shade to part sun

Golden ragwort is one of the first spring wildflowers, making a great show as a tall, exuberant plant. The abundant early spring blooms are very showy, bright yellow, with daisylike heads, borne in flat-topped arrays. It is a slowly spreading colony from handsome, rounded, evergreen leaves. It can create an evergreen mass in virtually any light and soil situation, from average to moist or boggy. It doesn't mix well with other plants, but let it have the whole show. Golden ragwort is easy to thin out as it tries to escape its assigned area.

*syn. *Senecio aureus*

Phlox divaricata

woodland phlox

rich woods

spring, summer, fall, winter

1 ft., spreading

shade to part sun

For a few short weeks in early spring, woodland phlox can form a dense mass of very fragrant, butterfly-attracting blue flowers on 1 ft. stems. The plant is remarkably easy to grow and divide. It can mix with other equally robust wildflowers, as its low-growing, creeping stems with 1 in. long, dense evergreen leaves do not form an impenetrable mat. It is an effective ground cover all year. Several selections are available: 'Clouds of Perfume' is light blue; 'Fuller's White' is pure white; 'London Grove Blue' has lilac-blue flowers.

Phlox stolonifera

creeping phlox

rich woods

spring

8 in., spreading

part shade to part sun

Creeping phlox is a captivating garden plant with leafy stolons that run along the ground, growing a foot or more each year and producing a patch of evergreen foliage. The growth will be lusher in rich, less-acid conditions, so consider adding a little lime. The almost leafless flowering stems rise 6–8 in. come spring, bearing striking clusters of slightly larger trumpetlike flowers that are not as dense as woodland phlox. Selections include 'Blue Ridge' and 'Pink Ridge'. 'Bruce's White' is one of the very best; 'Sherwood Purple', with mauve-purple flowers, is very popular.

Podophyllum peltatum

mayapple

bottomlands and rich woods

spring

1 × 1 ft., creeping

shade to part sun

Mayapple is a very popular native plant, reminding some people of their childhood playgrounds "down by the creek." It grows easily to form an attractive expanse of large leaves and is not fussy about soil conditions. The 1–2 in. wide flowers are showy but hidden beneath the paired leaves. The fruit is a single, large, fleshy, egg-shaped berry, turning yellow when ripe in late summer; it is fun for children to look for these "hidden" treasures. Because of its robust underground stems, mayapple can become invasive and should not be grown with other wildflowers; it is best by itself in a woodland area or floodplain. Mayapple requires no care and may die down in mid- to late summer in dry conditions. It looks great when the leaves are just emerging in spring, with their green shine and just-forming flower buds. Spend some time watching them emerge.

Polemonium reptans

Jacob's-ladder

rich woods

spring, summer

1 × 1 ft.

shade to part shade

This favorite is a long-lasting spring wildflower with beautiful light blue flowers on a clumping plant with medium-textured leaves. It appears delicate, but Jacob's-ladder is adaptable and fits in well with other wildflowers. You can't have too many—its foliage lasts well into summer and helps keep the wildflower garden looking good. But be aware, the variegated selections are not heat tolerant and are best in the mountains.

Polygonatum biflorum*

large Solomon's-seal

rich woods

spring, summer, fall

2–6 × 2–3 ft.

light shade to part sun

Large Solomon's-seal quickly grows into a large colony from deep underground rhizomes. Its tall, leafy stems are robust and conspicuous, even showstopping on larger specimens, producing clusters of three 1 in. wide flowers hidden under each leaf. Next come purple berries that aren't visible until the leaves wither in fall; birds often find these berries irresistible. The plant provides unexcelled structural form because all the stems seem to arch in the same direction, and the leaves are droopy, playing off the light. The largest forms, with leaves to 6 ft. tall, are often sold as giant Solomon's-seal. These forms are impressive by any name and a wonder to behold. The common name refers to the large, round, pitted scar left by the leaf on the top of the rhizome.

*syn. *P. commutatum*

Primula meadia*

shooting-star

rich woods

spring

1–2 × 1 ft.

part shade to part sun

This may be the most elegant plant in your spring garden. It sports graceful white flowers hanging down in an umbrellalike cluster on tall stalks, from a basal clump of bright green leaves. Each flower looks like a primrose whose petals have been blow-dried backward, exposing the yellowish stamens for pollination. Watch the bumblebees visit, hang upside down on the tip, and buzz at different frequencies to vibrate the pollen out of the stamens. The spring flowers are short lived, but the plants are long lived. Don't feel bad when they die down completely in early summer; this allows them to avoid hot weather, like swans migrating north. The forms in the western part of the country are pink and not heat tolerant in the Southeast.

*syn. *Dodecatheon meadia*

Ruellia caroliniensis

Carolina wild-petunia

open woods and grassy areas

spring, summer, fall

1 × 1 ft.

shade to part sun

A charming little plant, Carolina wild-petunia seems to delight in Piedmont open woodlands, among grasses, on shady banks, and along disturbed paths in various soils, tolerating drought and heat. It grows to 1 ft., producing 1½ inch, trumpetlike, light blue to pinkish white flowers, with new blooms opening every day all summer. Take time to smell the wild-petunias, and delight in these little gems that self-sow and take care of themselves. They are difficult to pull up and move (they break off easily), so leave them be. You just might have some already in your backyard woods. Likely not for taming in the bed or border, Carolina wild-petunia flowers are, however, fun for children to pick.

Sanguinaria canadensis

bloodroot

woods

spring, summer, fall

6 × 6 in.

shade to part shade

Perhaps our most prized wildflower, bloodroot is well known and easy to grow. Its value in the wildflower garden cannot be overstated. This cheerful harbinger of spring forms discrete clumps from thick, finger-sized rhizomes that have red sap. Each large, white flower emerges, pristine and disproportionately large, surrounded by a single unfurling leaf. The joy this brings is likened to viewing a newborn child. Seeds are abundantly produced and readily self-sow in a woodland garden. Eventually, the seeds can produce dozens of ever-enlarging clumps and produce a dazzling display of late winter flowers that can resemble a light snowfall. The handlike, lobed leaf is unique and attractive as summer foliage. The seeds are attractive to woodland ants, who carry them away like groceries; curious kids can collect fresh seeds from the 2 in. long pods, put them in a pile on the ground, and watch the show.

Sedum ternatum

mountain stonecrop

rich woods and rocky ledges

spring, summer, fall, winter

3 × 6 in.

light shade to part sun

One of only a handful of sedums that love shade, mountain stonecrop makes a great ground cover in thin soil over rocks and in walls where other plants would not thrive. Because the loosely mat-forming stems are so brittle and delicate, this plant can be overlooked by those designing a woodland garden. However, it can be a great addition in the right niche, especially if it is watered during droughts. It is a joy to see the clusters of starry white flowers on diminutive, leafy, evergreen stems growing on a mossy rock.

Solidago caesia

wreath goldenrod

dryish woods

fall

1–3 × 1–2 ft.

part shade to part sun

Wreath goldenrod is a reliable performer in light woodland shade, flowering beautifully in late summer into fall, even when dry. The attractive yellow blooms are in small clusters on arching stems with bluish green leaves. Wreath goldenrod is an excellent pollinator plant for autumn. The clumps slowly enlarge and are never dominating.

Spigelia marilandica

Indian-pink

dryish woods

spring, summer

1.5 × 1.5 ft.

part shade to part sun

Indian-pink is certainly one of our best and most striking wildflowers. A big clump in bloom is a showstopper, and it gets better with age. The tubular flowers are very showy, scarlet and yellow, opening one at a time per stalk, blooming in late spring and sporadically later, especially attractive to hummingbirds. The fruit is a heart-shaped pod with 2 seeds, maturing sporadically in summer; the trick is to catch the seeds before they pop out when you're not looking. The seeds you miss will sow themselves where they fall and sprout readily. The plants are adaptable to various light levels, but do not like hot sun. Keep Indian-pink moist for best growth, and cut bloomed-out stems back halfway for sporadic reblooming.

Stylophorum diphyllum

woods poppy

rich woods

spring

1 × 1 ft.

part shade to part sun

Woods poppy, also called celandine poppy, is luscious when the large, showy yellow flowers begin to open in early spring. They bloom well longer than many spring wildflowers, but their leaves lose their pleasing appeal by summer. All parts of the plant have a yellow-colored sap when broken. The fruit themselves are more interesting than most—1 in. long pods covered with touchable, long, white, rough hairs splitting open in late spring. The seeds ripen early and bountifully self-sow. Woods poppy grows from a knotty root that you can dig and divide; move the extra plants around or give them away.

Tiarella wherryi

foamflower

rich woods

spring, summer, fall, winter

1 × 1 ft.

shade to part sun

A most satisfying wildflower, foamflower produces very attractive, starlike flowers on short stalks arising from neat, leafy evergreen clumps. It is a must-have for any wildflower venue. Use it liberally, as edging, in groupings, as ground cover, and to provide attractive companion specimens during the summer doldrums with your ferns. If plants wilt, you know it's time to water everything. Many nifty if atypical-looking hybrids and cultivars have been created, providing new forms and colors. Some may do better in cooler climes. 'Dark Eyes' has burgundy leaf markings. 'Iron Butterfly', 'Neon Lights', and 'Oakleaf' have deeply lobed leaves and colorful markings. 'Spring Symphony' is probably the best all-around selection for toughness and beauty. Heartleaf foamflower (*Tiarella cordifolia*) is a spreading ground cover with runners. It produces a carpet of leaves and abundant flowers arising from the mass of growth. Selections and hybrids abound.

Trillium cuneatum

sweet Betsy trillium

rich woods and bottomlands

spring, summer

1 × 1 ft.

shade to part shade

Trilliums as a group are the jewels of the spring garden, and like gems, they come in a range of colors, shapes, and sizes. They all have three leaves on a single stem, from a thick tuberlike rhizome, and the flowers are either stalkless or stalked. We have transplanted trillium in bloom; that means they're adaptable. Sweet Betsy trillium is a favorite because the leaves have gorgeous mottled patterns. The plant is very easy to grow and self-sows readily if you start with 2–3 plants that can cross-pollinate to make seeds. It is prone to clumping. Other desirable stalkless trilliums vary slightly in flower color but are more difficult to acquire. Chattahoochee trillium (*Trillium decipiens*) is our favorite, with maroon flowers and leaves that are spectacularly mottled in shades of green and purple, as is Underwood's trillium (*T. underwoodii*). Decumbent trillium (*T. decumbens*) has red-maroon flowers with longer petals.

Trillium flexipes

bent white trillium

rich woods

spring

1 × 1 ft.

part shade to part sun

This species is a good representative of the stalked trillium group. Bent white trillium is robust, with pure white flowers on 1–2 in. tall stalks held above the leaves. The leaves are almost never mottled, can be very wide, and may die down in summer. Another stalked trillium that performs well in the Southeast is Catesby's trillium (*Trillium catesbaei*), with alluring pink flowers. While the much-loved classic white trillium, *T. grandiflorum*, is beautiful, it and many red trillium species (such as *T. erectum*) are not heat tolerant, so we recommend bent white trillium as a selection that will not disappoint southeastern gardeners. A gorgeous species that also cannot be grown outside its cool, acidic mountain habitat is painted trillium (*T. undulatum*). While very tempting and frequently offered for sale, it is not garden worthy in the South; we can enjoy its beauty in its native haunts along the Blue Ridge Parkway.

Trillium luteum

yellow trillium

rich woods

spring

1 × 1 ft.

shade to part shade

Unique in having both bright yellow flowers and a sweet lemony fragrance, yellow trillium is a classic giant trillium of the Smoky Mountains. It can have leaves over 1 ft. wide and makes clumps. The light green, mottled leaves fit in well with larger spring wildflowers. Similarly, mottled trillium (*Trillium maculatum*) is fruity smelling and has red-maroon flowers with petals that are wider toward the tips. The leaves are marked by exquisite mottling. Like many species of this genus, mottled trillium dies down by early summer—one way to beat the heat. Twisted trillium (*T. stamineum*), also known as helicopter toadshade (Larry's favorite common name), has maroon flowers with twisted petals that are splayed out flat to reveal the maroon stamens as the showiest part of the flower. This whimsical-looking species readily forms clumps and is a favorite of children.

Trillium recurvatum

prairie trillium

floodplains and meadow edges

spring, summer

1 × 1 ft.

part shade to part sun

Prairie trillium grows in moist, open areas of the Upper Southeast, with small leaves, very wide and pointed red-maroon petals, and sepals that flex downward. It also characteristically spreads via underground rhizomes, to create a diffused patch that can last longer into the summer than other species. It is easy to identify, grow, and proliferate. Lanceleaf trillium (*Trillium lancifolium*) is the only other trillium species that readily forms colonies by underground proliferation. Lanceleaf's narrow, mottled leaves grow atop thin stems, and its flowers have narrow, spirally twisted petals that look like dark candle flames. It dies down early, but is a delicate addition to the spring garden.

Uvularia grandiflora

large bellwort

rich woods

spring, summer

1 × 1 ft.

shade to part sun

Large bellwort is a terrific plant, pushing its way up quickly and showing color in the earliest days of spring. The stems and leaves appear to have just come out of the washing machine and are twisted and wrinkled, but that's part of the charm—they straighten out later. The 1 in. wide, bright yellow flowers emerge from the leaves and last a short time. As the plant matures, it becomes a spacious clump and offers attractive foliage into summer. It is long lived, forming satellite clumps and lasting for years. Seek out this less common bellwort.

Sun-Loving Perennials

Perennials are those plants that come back and bloom every year after you plant them, hopefully bigger and better. In making selections for your sunny border or pollinator garden, follow the normal aspects of design and put taller behind smaller. Consider choosing a mix of species that will give you continuous flowers from early summer to late fall. Don't forget to include plants that supply food to butterfly larva—they may not contribute showy blooms but are necessary for the life cycles of important pollinators. Leave seed heads up as long as you can for birds to eat seeds and insects to utilize the stems. The perennial garden will need periodic (not necessarily yearly) attention to thin out and divide for plant rejuvenation, or to discard poor performers. Plant what you like, enjoy what you see, plan for new additions, and call the important pollinating activities of bees, hummingbirds, and butterflies to the attention of visitors to your garden.

Agastache scrophulariifolia

purple giant-hyssop

rich woods and bottomlands

summer, fall

2–5 × 2–3 ft.

part sun to sun

The hyssops are classic garden annuals for the sunny border, attracting a myriad of interesting visitors for the rich nectar. They are in the mint family, so the stems are square and the foliage is usually aromatic. There are many species, mostly in western states, and many garden hybrids, providing some cultivars with lush, brightly colored flowers. They generally bloom all summer and can make handsome specimens—cut back spent flower heads to keep them blooming. Our native giant-hyssop has lavender to purple flowers in dense spikes, sitting atop leafy clumping plants. It blooms midsummer through fall and is fragrant. Do not overwater or it will become too lush. Save seeds or buy new plants each year; some seeds may self-sow and continue in your garden. The larger forms can be for the back of the border, the smaller are nice massed in front.

Ageratina altissima*

white snakeroot

moist woods and roadsides

late summer, fall

2–4 × 2–3 ft.

part sun to sun

This is a wonderful species that covers itself with long-lasting, tiny white flowers in dense clusters in the late summer to fall. Its lush, medium-textured leaves are triangular. In the mountains, where it is very common, white snakeroot is a sign of late summer and can be prolific along roadsides. It can seed itself around the garden in cooler climes, but barely tolerates our warm, humid summers. The cultivar 'Chocolate', with dark purple foliage and snow-white flowers, is striking. The foliage is darker in full sun, but may need afternoon protection farther south.

*syn. Eupatorium rugosum

Allium cernuum

nodding onion

open woods and rock outcrops

summer

1 × 1 ft.

part sun to sun

This attractive wild onion is more of a northern prairie species; its globose heads of pink blooms are beautiful in early summer. It is barely tolerant of our hot summers outside the mountains, but this may help keep it in check, as it can spread by its proliferating bulbs (not edible). Do not overwater, just let it die down in the meadow or perennial border. Nodding onion can produce striking flowers that bees love. It looks great in bloom with orange butterfly-weed, and the dried seed heads can be left for ornament. It is easy to grow and may naturalize in a sunny rock garden.

Amsonia hubrichtii

threadleaf bluestar

prairie meadows

spring, summer, fall

3 × 3–4 ft.

sun

Threadleaf bluestar is one of the must-have perennials for the sunny border. It comes from the western prairies just beyond our range, but is quite happy and drought tolerant in the Southeast in a variety of well-drained soils. It grows from a tough woody rootstock, difficult to divide, so plant it where you want it forever, give it some room, and then leave it alone. It makes a magnificent clump of narrow foliage that looks great all summer, especially as a background for other perennials; and then surprisingly has the finest golden yellow fall color of any perennial. Even if it didn't produce beautiful light blue spring flowers, we would still plant it for the summer form and fall color.

Amsonia tabernaemontana

common bluestar

moist woods and stream edges

spring, summer

2–4 × 2–4 ft.

part shade to sun

Common bluestar is a long-lived perennial, robust in the garden, that produces beautiful blue flowers for a short period in spring. Sometimes there is more leaf than flower, especially if the plants is in too much shade, but it looks good as a foliage plant all summer. It likes full sun, but appreciates some afternoon shade in the Deep South. The excellent cultivar 'Blue Ice' and the floriferous variety *montana* are smaller. The more delicate sandhills bluestar (*Amsonia ciliata*), from the sandy soils of the Coastal Plain, is also more heat and drought tolerant, with very narrow, hairy leaves and smaller flowers.

Antennaria virginica

shale barren pussytoes

dry, rocky habitats

spring, summer, fall

4–6 in. tall, spreading

part shade to part sun

This is a new garden plant on the scene, from the hilly shale barren habitats of Virginia and West Virginia. But what an impact it has made! It is a diminutive plant whose flower stalk is only 6 in. tall, topped with small, soft, creamy flower heads that are reminiscent of—you guessed it, little cat paws. The mass blooming in spring doesn't last long and the stalks all die away to leave a silvery gray crust of tight, ground-hugging foliage. This plant spreads by surface stems to form a tight carpet that is 1 in. thick. It creeps and crawls in a remarkable way, and can cover many square feet in 2–3 years. It can also be neatly trained in a rock garden setting. Once established, it loves dryish, rocky, or well-drained loamy soil in open shade, even tolerating full morning sun. Do not plant in humus-rich soil or overwater.

Asclepias incarnata

swamp milkweed

wetlands and marshes

summer

3–5 × 1–2 ft.

part sun to sun

Swamp milkweed is a very popular species with pink flowers, but there are rose-pink ('Cinderella') and pure white ('Ice Ballet') selections as well. It is a tall, multibranched leafy plant and, while it comes from native wetlands, it does just fine in ordinary garden soil if you provide supplemental watering during droughts. It blooms from late spring on, and if you cut it back by half in midsummer, it may regrow and bloom some more. Try it in rain gardens as it is quite tolerant. It may suffer from the persistent summer heat in the Deep South. Common milkweed (*Asclepias syriaca*), sometimes mistakenly called white milkweed, has sweet-smelling pink flowers in big, globose clusters; butterflies and Monarch caterpillars love it. But *A. syriaca* is very coarse and an aggressive spreader and not recommended for the garden—keep it in the wild meadow.

Asclepias tuberosa

butterfly-weed

meadows, roadsides, and dryish woods

summer, fall

1–2 × 1–2 ft.

part sun to sun

Butterfly-weed is a fabulous native, adapting to well-drained sites and blooming over a long period. It is a clumper, and magnificent large specimens can develop in the right conditions. The fleshy taproot grows deep, so plant it where you want it to stay forever and do not plan to move it. The flowers are orange to yellow and even (rarely) red, ½ in. long, in dense, flat-topped clusters, opening sequentially over a long period in early summer. The fruit is a long, hornlike pod to 4 in. long, maturing to split open and release masses of fluffy parachuted seeds—an occurrence children love. Warning: Do not open the ripe pods indoors or you'll have fuzz all over the floors. If cut back after late spring blooming, and watered during droughts, butterfly-weed will grow back and bloom some more. Do not overwater, though. It attracts many insects, especially monarch butterflies. A seed strain called 'Gay Butterflies' produces good plants in an array of bright colors.

Baptisia alba

white wild indigo

low meadows and woods

spring, summer

3–5 × 3–4 ft.

part sun to sun

Blooming in late spring and then forming attractive, huge leafy mounds, white wild indigo is a grand wildflower. It looks good all summer as a dense foliage plant in the sunny border and increases in size every year, so give it plenty of room. The new shoots look like emerging asparagus spears and are interesting in their own right. The pea-like flowers in their formal spikes are spectacular when a large clump is in bloom. Plant other perennials nearby for summer color. Good white selections are 'Wayne's World' and 'Ivory Towers'.

Baptisia australis

blue false indigo

riverbanks and meadows

3–5 × 2–3 ft.

spring, summer

sun

There are many baptisia species and hybrids from which to choose, both tall and short, in a range of colors. Blue false indigo (*Baptisia australis*) is a tall plant, with beautiful dark blue flowers. Its leaves are darker than those of white wild indigo. The hybrid of *B. alba* and *B. australis*, 'Purple Smoke', was discovered as a chance seedling at the North Carolina Botanical Garden about 1990. It is a fabulous plant, 5–6 ft. tall, producing numerous, robust, smoky purple flowers with gray-green leaves. Of equal beauty is the tall 'Carolina Moonlight', a hybrid with a profusion of soft yellow flowers. For a bright splash, try 'Screaming Yellow', with outlandish yellow flowers on tall, robust plants. Another outstanding yellow bloomer is 'Sunny Morning'. For smaller selections, check out the Decadence® series, with such names as 'Lemon Meringue' and 'Sparkling Sapphires'. Exceptional dwarf selections include 'Blueberry Sundae' and 'Dutch Chocolate'.

Boltonia asteroides

white doll's-daisy

marshes and ditches

summer

2–3 × 2–3 ft.

part sun to sun

White doll's-daisy is a very worthwhile plant for the mid- to late-summer border. Its long-blooming, charming, daisylike flowers, white with a yellow center, are produced in multibranched profusion on a delicate plant with narrow leaves. It fits in well with other tall, medium-textured plants. It will outperform itself if given a little extra water. The clump slowly enlarges and will eventually need dividing, which is easy to accomplish. The common cultivar 'Snowbank' is highly recommended over the standard—it is a bit smaller and neater, with bluish green leaves.

Callirhoe papaver

poppy mallow

pine woods and barrens

spring, summer, fall

1 × 3–4 ft.

part sun to sun

Also known as wine cup, woodland poppy mallow produces an amazing floral display in the garden—eye-popping, bright magenta flowers on a flourish of toothy cut foliage. It is a native perennial from dryish habitats in the Deep South, but has been shown to be very adaptable in the garden in a variety of soils and light conditions. Good sun and average, well-drained soil is best, however. Woodland poppy mallow sprawls to form an informal mass, blooming heavily in spring and then sporadically all summer into fall. It is also adaptable to containers if you don't overwater. The bright colors add a sparkle to summer gardens. Other, more western, species may work well, too, such as *Callirhoe involucrata*.

Chelone glabra

white turtlehead

moist woods, streambanks

late summer

2–3 × 1–2 ft.

part shade to sun

White turtlehead is a surprising plant; its flowers are shaped like a turtle's head stretching out of its shell, with a mouth even, tightly arranged in a 4-ranked cluster atop thick-textured, leafy stems. It forms a slowly enlarging colony, easy to manage and thin out. Pink turtlehead (*Chelone lyonii* 'Hot Lips') has bright pink flowers on short, leafy stems. *Chelone glabra* 'Black Ace' has dark purple leaves. As you can imagine, since *chelone* means "tortoise" in Greek, stories of turtles and mythology abound. It is fun to watch the bees force their way into the flower "mouths."

Clinopodium coccineum*

scarlet calamint

sandy pinewoods

summer, fall, winter

1–2 × 1–2 ft.

sun

Striking, 1½ in. wide, tubular red flowers dominate scarlet calamint in bloom, and this beautiful, open, evergreen subshrub blooms almost continuously. It requires full sun and perfect drainage, preferably a sand pile or open, gravelly rock garden setting. It is really a shrub, with wiry twigs that add new growth every year. Because it is so delicate, though, we treat it with the perennials, and it does not die down in winter. It mixes well with other fine-textured, twiggy subshrubs (such as the herbs rosemary, thyme, and sage). 'Amber Blush' and 'Ohoopee Yellow' are lovely yellow-flowered cultivars. As a group, these plants may be referred to as the shrub mints, and they are best grown in the Deep South. Related to this species, but quite different looking, is Georgia calamint (*Clinopodium georgianum*), a smaller shrub 1–2 ft. tall, with rounded, minty smelling leaves and prolific, bright pink, rosemarylike flowers in late summer.

*syn. Calamintha coccinea, Satureja coccinea

Conoclinium coelestinum*

hardy ageratum

moist ditches

fall

2–3 × 2 ft.

part sun to sun

Hardy ageratum is a welcome plant for color in late summer and until frost. It is also a veritable bee and butterfly magnet and is very attractive when in full bloom. The tiny blue-purple flowers are aggregated into tight clusters. However, it is a proliferating spreader (by seeds and runners) and needs to be controlled in the garden. We let it grow and just pull it up as it fades or get in the way. It is wonderful to have around when most everything has declined, or in tough wet or dry places where nothing else will grow.

*syn. Eupatorium coelestinum

Coreopsis auriculata

mouse-ear coreopsis

open woods

spring, summer, fall, winter

1 × 2 ft.

part sun to sun

Mouse-ear coreopsis is part of a large group of long-blooming, daisylike, yellow-flowered coreopsis species that span a variety of habitats—from shade to sun. They make great garden plants. Typically, they can be recognized by their conspicuous petal tips that feature 3 to 5 notches. Mouse-ear coreopsis is a tall species in the wild, but is best represented in the garden by its delightful cultivar 'Nana', a dwarf selection. 'Nana' forms an excellent semievergreen ground cover that is 2 in. tall and blooms heavily in spring, producing bright yellow-orange flowers on 8 in. tall stalks. This is one of our all-time favorites.

Coreopsis lanceolata

longstalk coreopsis

open woods

summer

2 × 2 ft.

part sun to sun

Longstalk coreopsis is a common clump-forming perennial with stiffly erect stems and long leaves. It is often crossed with the similarly large-flowered *Coreopsis grandiflora* to make many garden hybrids, such as 'Tequila Sunrise' (yellow with a red blotch in the flower's center); 'Sunkiss' (with deeper notched petals); and Uptick® (with a maroon center). All these may behave more as short-lived perennials in the warm South.

Coreopsis palustris

swamp tickseed

wetlands

summer, fall, winter

1–2 × 2 ft.

part sun to sun

Swamp tickseed is by far best represented in the garden with the cultivar 'Summer Sunshine', developed at the Mt. Cuba Center in Delaware. The foliage is dense and sturdy and resistant to devastating powdery mildew disease. Striking yellow flowers bloom abundantly in September and October on a clumping plant. This beauty is a welcome site before the fall asters begin.

Coreopsis pubescens

star tickseed

open woods

spring, summer, fall, winter

1–2 × 2–3 ft.

part sun to sun

Tickseed is just another common name for various core-opsis, a large and varied group with many great garden plants. Most have 1–2 in. wide bright flowers in the yellow range, often with maroon marking; many are short-lived perennials in the warm South. They are worth growing anyway. Hairy tickseed (*Coreopsis pubescens*) is best represented by the compact, dazzling superstar 'Sunshine Superman'. In its first year in a sunny, well-drained site, it can literally bloom all summer into fall if provided supplemental water. Tall coreopsis (*C. tripteris*) grows to 8 ft. or more, forming a large, spreading clump with many gray-green, 3-parted leaves and huge clusters of 2–3 in. wide flowers in midsummer. For that roomy spot in the sunny garden, its larger-than-life size is excellent. 'Gold Standard' tall coreopsis is a little shorter and long lived.

Coreopsis verticillata

threadleaf coreopsis

dryish woods

summer, fall

1–2 × 2 ft.

part sun to sun

This selection is widely known and grown, mostly for its airy foliage and long bloom all summer. It forms a mound with threadlike leaves and pretty yellow flowers. It is often used as a ground cover in front of taller specimens. Good cultivars in various yellow shades include 'Zagreb', which is the gold standard as a tight, compact coreopsis; 'Golden Gain' and 'Golden Showers' are a bit taller, to 2 ft.

Cuthbertia rosea*

common roseling

mesic woods

summer, fall

1 × 1 ft.

part shade to part sun

Roseling is one of the newer members of the spiderwort clan to come into cultivation. As a garden plant, it is much subtler than spiderwort (*Tradescantia*). It is loosely clump forming, with short stems and arching, grasslike leaves. The delicate pink, 1 in. wide flowers can bloom from spring through the entire summer with a little supplemental water during droughts. We consider roseling a real winner in its own delicate way.

*syn. *Callisia rosea*

Echinacea purpurea

purple coneflower

open woods and dry roadsides

summer

2–4 × 1–2 ft.

part sun to sun

Coneflowers are a beautiful mainstay of the sunny border. The flowers are what you want in a strikingly showy perennial: large heads and pink-purple "petals" (ray flowers), held horizontally to slightly drooping; the central portion is tough and solid, becoming conelike in maturity. It blooms in summer; keep it cut back and it may keep blooming. Coneflowers mature soon after flowering, producing many flattened, thistlelike seeds in the heads that are relished by goldfinches. The species was once a mainstay in the home medicinal garden. Few of the colorful hybrid selections thrive in our hot southeastern gardens. Plant in well-drained soil and hope for the best. Cultivar 'Kim's Knee High' has gorgeous purple flowers on a shorter plant. Cultivar 'White Swan' has done poorly for us. We like the Tennessee coneflower (*Echinacea tennesseensis*) cultivar 'Rocky Top', with bold pink ray flowers that often flair upward. Pale purple coneflower (*E. pallida*) has some heat and drought tolerance.

Eryngium yuccifolium

rattlesnake master

prairies, barrens, glades, and woods

summer, fall

3–4 × 1–2 ft.

sun

We don't know whether the origin of this plant's common name, rattlesnake master, refers to using the plant to treat snakebite (likely), or perhaps to kill snakes. Folks could certainly do the latter, because of the tough, knobby floral heads they form, unique among wildflowers and striking en masse in the sunny garden. The basal leaves are yuccalike, but not sharply spiny. It attracts the most interesting array of insects as the white flowers appear from the heads, such that you and the children will be out there looking to see how many different ones you can see. Rattlesnake master prefers dryish, sandy soils kept moist, but not overwatered, in practically full sun. Try it in a rain garden.

Erythrina herbacea

coral bean

sandy woods and openings

summer, fall, winter

3–12 × 3–5 ft.

part sun to sun

Unique in its growth form, coral bean is reminiscent of its more tropical relatives that can grow to become trees. It is an herbaceous perennial in the colder Carolinas, becoming a woody shrub farther south and west into Texas. It is very late to sprout from the ground in spring, so don't give up too soon. The flowers are most unusual for a member of the bean family—tubular and bright red, attractive to hummingbirds. The bean pod fruit opens to reveal showy red seeds, lasting all winter into the following spring. The leaflets are distinctly lobed, narrow at each end and very wide in the middle. Be careful of the small rose-thorn prickles. Coral bean does not love shade, but will grow and flower in open woods. In well-drained soil, it makes a stunning clump 3–6 ft. across. In bloom, it's a showstopper for you and the hummingbirds. This species hybridizes with *Erythrina crista-galli* to form *E. ×bidwillii*, a 5–8 ft. floriforous subshrub with stunning red flowers.

Eupatorium perfoliatum

boneset

streambanks and moist woods

summer

2–4 × 2–3 ft.

part sun to sun

Neat and clean, boneset is a choice plant, adding stately form to sunny borders. Its rough texture is fun to feel. It loves a moist, sunny spot, but don't overwater it in rich soil or it will get too big and fall over. Broad heads of tiny white flowers bloom all summer. The fused leaves connect around the stem, a distinctive trait that led to the historical belief that it could mend broken bones. Try it in a rain garden. There are other varieties of boneset, but this one is the most ornamental.

Eutrochium species

Joe-pye weed

moist woods and marsh edges

summer

4–6 × 1–2 ft.

part sun to sun

Joe-pye weed (supposedly named after an 18th-century Native American medicine man) can be a giant—conspicuous in mid- to late summer in average or moist to wet habitats, where its multistemmed clumps rise above other herbaceous vegetation. It is a butterfly magnet, with big heads of small pink flowers. The leaves are distinctly whorled, with 4 to 7 in each ring, regularly spaced along the thick stems. If Joe-pye weed is too tall for your plot, cut the stem down by half in mid-June and it will regrow shorter and bushier. Three-nerved Joe-pye weed (*Eutrochium dubium*) has only 3–4 leaves per whorl, heavily spotted stems, and more delicate blooms. The cultivar 'Little Joe' is much smaller, at 2–3 ft. Spotted Joe-pye weed (*E. maculatum*) has the 4–5 ft. cultivar 'Gateway'. Tall Joe-pye weed (*E. fistulosum*) reaches 8–10 ft. in a moist garden, but you can plant one of the shorter cultivars such as 'Atropurpurea', which reaches only 7 ft.

Gaillardia pulchella

beach blanket flower

sandy soils in woods and dunes

summer

1 × 1 ft.

sun

Beach blanket flower is so colorful, it's as if it is already one of Mother Nature's garden selections. It likes well-drained, sandy soil and is especially prominent on beach dunes and sandy roadsides. It will grow better if you add coarse sand to your soil, and do not overwater. Heck, you could probably grow it in pure sand. And it must have full sun. Did we mention do not overwater? Try beach blanket flower as path edging, in rock gardens, and in containers—it should grow and bloom all summer. There are many selections that behave as colorful annuals; some are hybrids with western species. Seeing these at home may remind you of your beach trips—feel free to scatter some of the coarse sand on your sidewalk for full effect.

Helenium autumnale

dogtooth-daisy

moist meadows and woods

late summer, fall

2–4 × 2–3 ft.

sun

In late summer, dogtooth-daisy provides showy, long-lasting flowers that are well characterized by their yellow ray petals with 3 teeth. Plants become tall and may need staking if they are overfertilized and overwatered. There are many new cultivars that are shorter and stockier and feature shades of red and bronze. Try 'Butterpat', with golden yellow flowers; 'Helena Gold' and 'Helena Red', which are heat tolerant; or 'Moerheim Beauty', with dark red flowers. Purple-headed sneezeweed (*Helenium flexuosum*) is a summer-blooming native that grows 2–3 ft. tall, with winged stems; it is distinctive in that its central disk flowers are dark purple.

Helianthus angustifolius

swamp sunflower

wetlands and ditches

fall

3–10 × 2–4 ft.

sun

Sunflowers are signature plants of North America. They are very important for wildlife and humans as food. They are usually robust, both clump-forming and spreading species, blooming in late summer with their cheery big yellow flowers. The well-known species grown for ornament, seed, and oil is the annual sunflower, *Helianthus anuus*. With few exceptions, they all may best be grown in dry or moist meadows and rough areas outside the formal garden. Swamp sunflower is a beauty. Be aware of its urge to spread even more vigorously under garden conditions and keep it lean on fertilizer and water. Try the cultivar 'Low Down'. Beautifully floriferous briefly in late summer, with smaller, bright yellow flowers, it grows only 1–2 ft. tall, and works in dry to wet situations. Sunflowers that form slowly enlarging colonies include the small-headed sunflower *H. microcephalus* for the sunny meadow, and forest sunflower (*H. decapetalous*), best in light shade. Leave the maturing seed heads of all sunflowers for the birds.

Helianthus maximiliani

Maximilian's sunflower

prairies and meadows

fall

3–10 × 2–4 ft.

sun

This sunflower selection hails mostly from the western tall grass prairie. In the Southeast it is tolerant of our heat and humidity and makes a splashy plant in the fall. It seems to have more blossom than plant, as its large yellow flowers appear among dark green leaves. The leaves are distinctive in that they curve slightly inward along the edges. Like most sunflowers, this one wants to spread, but keep it in check with full sun, no extra water, and lean, well-drained soil.

Heliopsis helianthoides

ox-eye sunflower

forests and woodland borders

summer, fall

3–6 × 2–3 ft.

sun

Finally: a sunflower that does not spread underground (though it generates a few seedlings). Fabulous! Ox-eye sunflower is also more refined in leaf and form than other sunflowers, smaller and more adaptable to every sunny garden substrate—even clay and fertile soils. Plus, the beautiful yellow flowers bloom longer. A good 2–3 ft. cultivar is 'Summer Sun'. Highly recommended for all your short sunflower needs. You may still want to grow a tall giant sunflower for the impressive heads.

Hesperaloe parviflora

red yucca

dry southwestern shrub lands

spring, summer, fall

3–4 × 2–3 ft.

sun

Red yucca is not a true yucca; much less coarse and spiny. The gently arching flower stalks rise 3 ft. above the clump of thick, stiff, gray-green leaves that have interesting fibrous strands peeling along their edges—fascinating by themselves. The 1 in. wide flowers range from coral-pink to bright red hummingbird colors. They seem to bloom forever, a flower sporadically here and there. Look for conspicuous globose seed pods with flat black seeds that are easy to sprout. While this charming species is from the southwestern deserts, it has proven to be adaptable in well-drained and rocky soils here in the Southeast. It would be ideal in a rock garden mixed with like-minded plants—*not* leafy perennials—bringing something different to the garden experience.

Hibiscus coccineus

scarlet hibiscus

marshes, swamps, and swales

summer

4–8 × 2–3 ft.

part sun to sun

No wildflower is more striking than scarlet (or cardinal) hibiscus. The giant, 6 in. wide red flowers are showstoppers and have been garden favorites in the South for generations. It makes a large, multistemmed clump; cutting it down by half in June will keep it shorter, with more flowering branches. A new flower opens each day. Keeping the developing fruit picked will prolong flowering (true of many perennials). Butterflies love it, and you will, too. There is nothing quite like it in the world, and it has been used with several other species to make wonderful garden hybrids. Among albino forms, the white Texas star 'Summer Snow' has stunning, pure white flowers. Plants can grow to 6 ft. or more, though it is not as cold tolerant when grown in a pot.

Hibiscus moscheutos

rose mallow

marshes and wet meadows

summer

3–6 × 2–3 ft.

part sun to sun

Our native rose mallow, which some like to call marsh mallow, has been a favorite garden perennial for a long time. The giant, 4–6 in. wide, red, pink, or white flowers and handsome foliage present an attractive show, but the plants do take up space and they become larger with age. Cutting them down by half on June 1 will shorten their stature and produce more flowering branches. Removing the seed pods will prolong blooming. Site rose mallow to receive abundant sunshine or it will weaken over time. It is adaptable to most soils and is a heavy feeder. Hybridization with other native hibiscus species (including *Hibiscus coccineus* and *H. moscheutos*) has produced an array of hardy cultivars. The classic 'Lady Baltimore' (pink) and 'Lord Baltimore' (red) have large, bright flowers with broad-lobed, rich green leaves. The famous 'Kopper King' has beautiful pink flowers and dark foliage.

Kosteletzkya pentacarpos*

seashore mallow

coastal dune swales and tidal marshes

late summer

3–4 × 2–3 ft.

sun

Seashore mallow is a magical plant. All who see it are mesmerized to stop and look. There is a special charm in this stately clumping plant, so symmetrical and perfect in form. The leaves and bright pink flowers complement each other in proportion. Butterflies and bees love it. It adds greatly to the late summer garden color (which can often use a colorful boost), and should be used more often. As with its hibiscus relatives, it is difficult to transplant and may produce copious seedlings.

*syn. K. virginica

Liatris spicata

gayfeather

prairies and moist meadows

summer

2–3 × 1 ft.

sun

Gayfeather, 2–3 ft. tall, is clump forming, from an underground crown with tuberous swellings. Its leaves are narrow and grasslike, 3–6 in. long, thick along the lower stem and gradually reducing upward. Gayfeather produces stiffly upright, wandlike flower stalks that are visually appealing and good for cutting. Crowd several clumps for best display. The showy, bright pink or purple to white flowers are in small heads clustered tightly along the stems. Not fussy about well-drained soils, *Liatris*, aka blazing-star, are ideal in the perennial border. Cut back halfway after flowering. There are many species and selections; the shorter 'Kobold' is the most well known. Blazing-star (*Liatris aspera*) has fabulous bushy flower wands. Appalachian blazing-star (*L. microcephala*) has countless little flowering stems and is drought tolerant. Spreading liatris (*L. squarrulosa*) naturally grows in dry open woods with basal, gray-green leaves. It sports large individual flower heads about 1 in. wide.

Lilium michauxii

Carolina lily

meadows, dryish woods, rocky hills

summer

1–2 ft. × 6 in.

part shade to part sun

Lilies are considered the most regal of wildflowers, and yet our natives are among the most difficult to grow. They arise from large, scaly bulbs deep underground, and do not like disturbance. Carolina lily, with 1–3 (usually only 1) pendulous flowers sporting flared back petals, is more heat tolerant and should accept any well-drained garden soil in morning sun. It is said to be the only fragrant lily in eastern North America, and the butterflies know it. It is hard to resist the tall orange Turk's-cap lilies (*Lilium superbum*) of the cool, high mountains—but leave them there. Actually, we would stick to easily grown Asiatic lilies for the garden, and enjoy the native lilies in the wild.

Lobelia cardinalis

cardinal flower

wet meadows, streambanks, low woods

summer

2–4 × 1 ft.

part shade to part sun

Cardinal flower is so widely recognized, it could be our national wildflower. It is the quintessential flower for attracting hummingbirds—so beautiful that you can sit and stare at it for hours. If you do, you will see a hummingbird visit every five minutes (maybe the same one). The bright red, 2 in. wide flowers adorn the upper half of the plant, and it keeps producing them all summer as the stem elongates. We have seen stems up to 8 ft. tall in rich, moist soils. It is very adaptable to a variety of growing conditions, light shade or part sun, and often forms multiple stems. While it may be short lived in dry spots, clumps of cardinal flower can be perennial if they are provided extra water. Watch for it to pop up from tiny seeds in moist sites.

Lysimachia ciliata

fringed loosestrife

moist woods

summer

1–2 × 1–2 ft.

shade to part sun

Fringed loosestrife—what a poetic name!—covers itself with ¾ in. wide bright yellow flowers and its leafy foliage makes a thorough ground cover in a variety of situations, wet to dry, sunny to shady. It is easily removed if it becomes too rambunctious with other perennials. The purple-leaved cultivar 'Firecracker' is exceptional as a sun-loving ground cover, its yellow flowers rising above the mounding, deep purple leaves. If it becomes untidy, simply cut back and it will resprout.

Monarda punctata

spotted horsemint

sandy habitats

summer

1–3 × 1–3 ft.

sun

Spotted horsemint (or spotted bee-balm) is a crazy-looking species from sandy coastal habitats. We love it! The white, gaping flowers with red spots sit above bright pink leaflets in several whorls on the stems, like pink nonpareils in a candy store. It is an annual and can reseed; the seedlings can be transplanted. Do not overwater. Grow it in very well-drained soil or pure sand and full sun—and watch the unbelievable play of insects through the summer. It is one of the best pollinator plants there is, even if its unconventional looks are not your cup of tea.

Monarda species

bee-balm

ditches, seeps, moist woods, streambanks

summer

2–4 × 1–2 ft.

part sun to sun

Bee-balm may be as famous for the medicinal Oswego-tea made from *Monarda didyma* as it is for its striking flowers and minty leaves. Hummingbirds, bees, and butterflies delight in the bright red flowers that appear in a tuft at the top of the tall plant. The semievergreen colony sends out fast-growing runners, ensuring a constant supply in the herb garden. Because it is so aggressive, this plant requires considerable attention to periodic division. Coming from the mountains and Upper South, it has poor heat tolerance, but don't overwater. There are selections and hybrids that offer improved heat tolerance and mildew resistance, such as 'Jacob Cline', which resists diseases and resembles the wild type. 'Mahogany' is shorter with wine-red flowers; Grand Marshall™ is shorter, but not dwarf. Wild bergamot (*M. fistulosa*) is a widespread prairie species with lovely pink flowers and soft, hairy stems. Hybrids of monarda abound and are all lovely.

Oenothera fruticosa

southern sundrops

dry meadows and woods

spring

1–2 × 1 ft.

sun

Southern sundrops is a delightful, clump-forming plant, good for massing and interplanting with other species (such as gayfeather, nodding onion, and beardtongue) for a mixed-meadow effect. Its bright yellow flowers are cheerful and prolific for a time in spring. Grow it in a well-drained, sunny location. There are several selections with red buds, including 'Fireworks'. The well-known spreading pink evening primrose (*Oenothera speciosa*) is a persistent species with large pink flowers that occurs in old gardens and neglected areas, widely naturalized from further west. Midwestern evening primrose (*O. pilosella*) has many large, 2 in. wide yellow flowers on 1–2 ft. tall leafy stems in late spring. It is an invasive spreader, forming leafy rosettes which must be left to overwinter for next spring flowering—do not cut back tops until these rosettes mature in summer. Keep plants on the dry side; if you get more than you need, they are easily removed.

*Oenothera gaura**

beeblossom

roadsides and woods

summer, fall

2–3 × 1–2 ft.

part sun to sun

Beeblossom, or gaura, is a delicate and wispy plant, its long, slender branches moving in the breeze, the loosely tethered white to pink flowers playing like small butterflies. This species has been used mostly as a fast-growing annual or biennial in wildflower mixes for quick meadows. Its relative from the Southwest, *Gaura lindheimeri*, sparked a rash of fabulous selections in recent decades to produce a surprising array of attractive selections. These whimsical cultivars are much more compact, vigorous, and heat tolerant than wild beeblossom, featuring large flowers in various shades of white to deep pink: 'Blushing Butterflies', 'Dauphin', 'Whirling Butterflies', and the most famous, 'Siskiyou Pink'. In all cases, don't overwater or overfertilize, and cut plants back after flowering to rejuvenate them. Most behave as short-lived perennials; all are fascinating in the garden.

*syn. *Gaura biennis*

Penstemon smallii

Small's beardtongue

cliffs, road banks, and dry woods

spring

1–2 × 1–2 ft.

part sun to sun

Small's beardtongue is the prettiest of the eastern, pink-flowered species and a must for the open woodland garden and half-sunny border. The soft, hairy foliage is handsome in itself, and the large, attractive flowers are tubular with 2-lipped mouths. Being a short-lived perennial, it gives one really good spring bloom and then perhaps one more spring from a tattered old plant. It's best to start new plants yearly or to encourage self-sowing, by having several plants to cross-pollinate. Tall white beardtongue (*Penstemon digitalis*) does excellent in the Southeast, with 2–3 ft. tall stems bearing 1 in. wide, flaring, white tubular flowers. The handsome basal green leaves are also a plus. Expect at least 2 years of bloom from these before decline. 'Dark Towers', with its bronze-red leaves, red stems, and tubular pinkish flowers, is sturdy, robust, and heat tolerant—a real knockout deserving a prominent location in the garden.

Phlox carolina

Carolina phlox

woods

spring, summer

1 × 1–2 ft.

part sun to sun

Common names for *Phlox carolina* include Carolina phlox, garden phlox, smooth phlox, and giant phlox. This group of medium to tall phloxes bloom in the spring to early summer and are excellent in the perennial border. The group includes *P. glaberrima*, known as smooth phlox. Their large heads of mostly pink, tubular-flaring, and sometimes fragrant blooms are good to have as early butterfly attractors. This is in contrast to the even more well-known mid- to late summer flowering species of tall garden phlox, *P. paniculata*. The best Carolina phlox cultivars, as determined by trials at the Mt. Cuba Center botanical garden, are 2–4 ft. pink 'Bill Baker', 'Kim', and 'Forever Pink'. Good *P. glaberrima* selections include 'Morris Berd' and 'N³ Springfall'. *Phlox maculata* 'Minnie Pearl' is pure white and wonderful.

Phlox nivalis

pineland phlox

dry woods and sandhills

spring, summer, fall, winter

4 in. × 1 ft.

part sun to sun

Pineland phlox, like other mat-forming phloxes, or thrift, provides a tight evergreen ground cover and boldly beautiful, dense masses of spring flowers in pinks and whites. It is adaptable to borders, path edging (though the clumps may rapidly enlarge), or open situations too rough or steep to manage with other plants. We have even seen low-growing phloxes treated like a lawn, mixed with grasses and mowed periodically. Grow them all in sun, and do not overwater. It may also be called trailing phlox. Cultivar 'Camla', with mauve-colored flowers, is very vigorous. Moss phlox, or creeping phlox (*P. subulata*) has shorter leaves and does very well on roadsides, hillsides, and well-drained sunny locations (especially in the cooler mountains), but they are quite acceptable for us in warmer climes. They come in many colors; try cultivar 'Candy Stripe'. Be careful: the other widely grown plant called "thrift" is really *Armeria maritima*, the sea thrift—they usually have problems with our heat and humidity; we don't recommend them.

Phlox paniculata

garden phlox

| streambanks, woods, and borders |
| summer |
| 2–4 × 1–2 ft. |
| sun |

Tall garden phlox is abundant along the Blue Ridge Parkway, sun-drenched roadsides, and moist ditches throughout the Upper South. It blooms in mid- to late summer and is a familiar mainstay of the sunny perennial border. Generally, it is 2–4 ft. tall. For many years, garden phlox has been bred and selected to produce showy, large clusters of consistently fragrant, bright flowers, some of which are unnaturally gaudy. The clumps enlarge slowly and are easy to grow and divide in most garden soils. Because of its severe susceptibility to powdery mildew disease, which disfigures the leaves, we are lucky to have many selections that are more disease resistant. 'Jeana' is a remarkable cultivar straight from the wild; it has smaller, deep-pink flowers in very dense clusters, is a butterfly favorite, everblooming, slow spreading, and absolutely mildewproof—a real garden winner. Other mildew-resistant, large-flowered, good bloomers include white 'Delta Snow', 'David', and 'Lavelle'. The latter is best for butterflies.

Physostegia virginiana

obedient plant

seeps and moist meadows

summer

2–3 × 2–3 ft.

part sun to sun

Obedient plant has been widely cultivated; it's a popular pass-along plant. It is quite pretty, produces abundant nectar, and is absolutely adaptable, but is usually too aggressive in the garden, where it lacks competition. Do not grow where it can overtake other plants—it will. The common name derives from the notion that the attractive, tubular, pink flowers—a favorite of hummingbirds—will stay pointed in one direction if you push them that way. But, guess what? They don't stay. (Just don't tell the kids.) 'Miss Manners' is one of several cultivars; it is white-flowered and a bit less aggressive.

Pycnanthemum incanum

silverleaf mountain mint

dry mountain woods and hillsides

summer

2–3 × 2–3 ft.

part shade to sun

Silverleaf mountain mint may be the best smelling mint you will find. The tiny white flowers are charming and delicate in tight terminal clusters, and their intricate structure may reveal dark spots and tufts of hairs. The fuzzy leaves are fun to hand someone to rub and smell. In close quarters the plant is invasive, sending out aggressive 3–4 ft. runners; we just pull out most of the extra plants each fall and let some grow back. In a meadow it is superb, showing off its white-topped leaves and flower clusters like snow on mountain trees. The flowers bloom all summer, attracting the most unusual bonanza of seldom-seen insects; beekeepers tell me it is a great drought-tolerant nectar plant in summer, when others have faded. Even better: it is deer resistant.

Pycnanthemum tenuifolium

slender mountain mint

meadows and forests

spring, summer

1–2 × 1–2 ft.

part sun to sun

Slender mountain mint is widespread, with a much-branched, flat-topped array of flowers and needlelike leaves. It is strongly clumping, has great texture, can grow in light shade or sun, and likes its soils dryish. A great combination of traits, plus it still has the fresh, minty, pycnanthemum smell, and attracts lots of insects. Slender mountain mint looks good in grassy meadow settings.

Ratibida pinnata

grayhead coneflower

prairies, thickets, woods

summer

3–6 × 2–3 ft.

sun

Grayhead coneflower is one of the hallmarks of a true Midwest prairie, growing in a few places in the Southeast. It will tolerate a wide range of soils, but does not like wet clay, where it grows too large and falls over; keep it on the dry side in well-drained soil or you may need to stake it. Its distinctive large, cheerful flowers with drooping yellow ray petals make it a favorite. The plants form large clumps and extend in height above many other perennials. Butterflies love the flowers, and birds love the seeds.

Rudbeckia fulgida

orange coneflower

meadows, roadsides

summer

1–2 × 1–2 ft.

sun

Orange coneflower is a well-known wildflower of roadside meadows, and a classic for sunny borders and pollinator gardens. We don't know of a better wildflower that says "summer." It is long blooming (6 weeks or more) with large, orange-yellow flowers on continuously growing, hairy stems; short runners form a colony of plants which are easily divided as necessary. Grow it in full sun with minimal water to retard aggressiveness. A well-known, larger-flowered cultivar is the taller and more robust 'Goldsturm' ("storm of gold" in German); it is the one most often grown. Try 'Early Bird Gold' or 'Little Goldstar', both are shorter. Butterflies and bees love the flowers, while goldfinches love the seeds—leave stems standing until the seeds are gone. Grow as much of this species as you can find room for in your garden.

Rudbeckia hirta

black-eyed Susan

prairies and dry meadows

summer

1–2 × 1–2 ft.

sun

Technically, this species is an annual or biennial with bristly, hairy stems and large, perky, yellow flowers with maroon markings. It makes a big show and does best in well-drained soil and full sun. Take care to not overwater. It is first rate as a pollinator plant. Small birds, such as goldfinches, like the seeds—so leave them up. There are countless cultivars, some with exceptionally large flowers. Try 'Cherry Brandy', with beautiful light maroon flowers; 'Cappuccino', whose blooms are dark orange with maroon centers; 'Prairie Sun', a tall cultivar with yellow flowers; 'Moreno', dwarf to 1 ft.; 'Irish Eyes', with narrow yellow petals on tall stems; 'Cherokee Sunset', fully double flowers in maroon and orange; and 'Prairie Glow', which produces dark orange flowers with yellow tips. All are described as deer resistant.

![Black-eyed Susan flowers with yellow petals and dark centers]

Rudbeckia laciniata

cutleaf coneflower

open woods and roadsides

summer

4–6 × 2–3 ft.

part shade to sun

This tall coneflower grows in shade or sun, moist or average soil. It becomes 6–8 ft. tall, with highly dissected leaves and a wonderful profusion of large, pale yellow flowers in late summer. Cutleaf coneflower is an imposing sight in the open shady garden or border. Deadhead after flowering to prevent a plethora of self-sown seedlings, or leave the seedheads for finches and sparrows. The cultivar 'Herbstsonne', the autumn sun coneflower, is a very robust, long-blooming clumper that grows to 8 ft. tall.

Rudbeckia maxima

giant coneflower

moist meadows

early summer

3–6 ft. × 1–3 ft.

sun

This species is truly a giant, and it really stands out in the garden. The leaves are very large and mostly basal, forming a slowly spreading clump. The tall, slender stems rise above most other plants, with bright, slightly drooping, yellow-orange ray flowers and brown central cones. Cut back stems and leaves after flowering and birds have gotten the seeds, or it will look a bit raggedy. Giant coneflower is drought resistant, and usually comes back looking fresh the following spring.

Rudbeckia subtomentosa

sweet coneflower

dry woods and prairies

summer

3–5 × 2–3 ft.

sun

Sweet coneflower is an amazing plant in the perennial border, growing 3–5 ft. tall and blooming profusely for 2 months. Its 4 in. wide, full yellow flowers are produced on a coarse, hairy plant that can be cut back earlier to produce a shorter stature. It is stunning and easy to grow, more compact than the spreading coneflowers. The distinctive cultivar 'Henry Eilers' is shorter and has petals rolled into a thin tube. Leave the old flowers a while for birdseed.

Rudbeckia triloba

three-lobed coneflower

dry woods

summer, fall

2–3 × 2–3 ft.

part shade to sun

Three-lobed coneflower, often know as brown-eyed Susan, is a many-branched, heat- and drought-tolerant plant that can take half shade as it grows in woodlands. It is beautiful in late summer and even into fall, covered in 1 in. wide yellow flowers with big brown centers—a choice species for the Southeast, and highly recommended. It will produce a few seedlings in the garden. You will love its profuse, 1 in. wide yellow flowers produced in abundance, and its neat, open growth form in light shade.

Salvia coccinea

scarlet sage

sandy openings

spring, summer, fall

1–2 × 1–2 ft.

sun

Scarlet sage is one of our splashiest and longest blooming (until frost) wildflowers. The plentiful flowers are bright red, tubular, and 2-lipped with lower lobes. It attracts hummingbirds and bees. Because it is an annual, you will need to start new plants each year or have self-sown seedlings coming along in sandy, well-drained soil. Give extra water in droughts, but do not overwater. Several good cultivars have been developed to use as bedding plants. 'Lady in Red' is bright red and 'Cherry Blossom' is white and salmon bicolored. The self-sown seedlings from these will revert to being more like the wild type (less compact and fewer flowers) after a few years, and would be lovely additions to a low-maintenance rock garden, flower bed, or meadow.

Salvia farinacea

mealycup sage

open, sandy sites

summer

1–3 × 1–2 ft.

part sun to sun

We do not have many garden-worthy sages (genus *Salvia*) in the Southeast—but many do come from Mexico. Most sages are best known as culinary or fragrant herbs from foreign lands. This species is from the Southwest, but it is tolerant of our extra rainfall in the Southeast. It is technically a perennial shrub, but is best used as an annual because of our cool, wet winters. Mealycup sage is tolerant of many soils as long as it is kept well drained and in sun. Use it as edging for borders and paths. The blue-green foliage forms a tidy mound, and the dark blue flowers are beautiful on numerous wandlike stems. You'll appreciate its great summer color.

Scutellaria incana

downy skullcap

open woods and margins

summer

2–3 × 1–2 ft.

part sun to sun

Able to hold its own with other perennials in the mixed border, downy skullcap is larger than most scullcaps. It is a multibranched but modest-textured perennial with hairy, gray-green-whitish foliage and terminal loose clusters of pretty blue flowers. In fact, it looks great rising above or with other equally textured specimens. It is long blooming, and will bloom some more if cut back after the main flowers are finished. In a shaded situation without companions, it would probably need staking and would not be seen as much of an addition. Other showy species include heartleaf skullcap (*Scutellaria ovata*), which is easy and floriferous, but spreads too much to suit us. A favorite is the Ocmulgee skullcap (*S. ocmulgee*) from south Georgia—an excellent garden perennial with rich, dark blue, 1 in. wide flowers on tall (1–2 ft.), dark green, leafy stems forming a modest clump in full sun.

Sisyrinchium angustifolium

blue-eyed grass

woods, meadows, roadsides

summer

1 × 1 ft.

part shade to part sun

Blue-eyed grass is a delicate plant with hardly any leaves, the stems being wide (winged) and taking over the function of the leaves. The blue, ½ in. wide flowers are charming, but small and sparse on the stem. New ones open every day. Used in masses or as path edging, it is terrific because of its strict clumping nature and ease of growth. It is also profuse and long blooming. Be forewarned, however: the flowers don't open until near noon. Larry took his field botany class out to a meadow to see blue-eyed grass flowers early one morning and none could be found. Where'd they go? When they came back a few hours later, all were in bloom. A good cultivar for the Southeast is 'Lucerne', a bright blue-purple. Try mixing it with clumping native bleeding-hearts along a shady border in late spring. It likes sun, but full hot sun during a dry summer is too much.

Solidago odora

licorice goldenrod

open woods and roadsides

summer

1–2 × 1–2 ft.

part sun to sun

Licorice goldenrod is a stately species, tightly clumped with a large head of bushy, flowering spikes forming a symmetrical plume. It has bluish green foliage, and the crushed leaves smell faintly like anise. This species is one of many goldenrods that produce full heads of yellow flowers in late summer. Some species spread vigorously; check the aggressiveness of your species before planting. Canada goldenrod (*Solidago canadensis*) is a robust (up to 5 ft. tall) species that forms discrete, rapidly spreading colonies in old fields, roadsides, and meadows. Beware of its tendency to take over. Stiff goldenrod (*S. rigida*) grows to 2 ft. tall and is stunning with a broad, flat-topped or rounded head of small flowers. Seaside goldenrod (*S. sempervirens*) comes from coastal dunes and is salt spray tolerant. It grows 4–6 ft. tall in a clump, with tall, branched plumes late into autumn. Goldenrod is especially attractive to pollinators and its sticky pollen does not cause hayfever.

Solidago rugosa

rough-stemmed goldenrod

meadows

fall

2 × 2 ft.

sun

Rough-stemmed goldenrod has small clusters of flowers on an array of branching stems. It requires full sun. An excellent cultivar is 'Fireworks'—you never saw so many tiny little flowers in one place! A single plant grows rapidly to form a dense colony with lush 2 in. long leaves near the ground, acting as a good semievergreen ground cover. It spreads readily and will need management if you grow it with other perennials (Larry discards 90 percent of his every year, and lets it regrow), but it can occupy a finite space (such as an island or space between sidewalks) and look great in late summer. *Solidago sphacelata* 'Golden Fleece' has long wands densely covered with flowers into autumn. It also grows in sun and is a slow spreader.

Stokesia laevis

Stokes' aster

bogs and pinelands

summer, fall, winter, spring

1–2 × 1–2 ft.

part sun to sun

Larry first saw Stokes' aster while he was standing in a wet pitcher plant bog in Alabama, grabbing a poison sumac branch for stability. The plant was beautiful. It is much anticipated in the summer garden because the heads are so large and the plants so robust (so much so that the flower stems often fall over if not staked). Its big, luscious blue flowers (like giant bachelor's buttons) have deeply lacerated petals. The clumps can grow large and informal, occupying some space, even prominent as winter foliage. Cut it back after flowering and it may bloom more later. We consider Stokes' aster a must-have for the garden. Several selections are improvements in tidiness. 'Peachie's Pick' is our favorite, its lavender flowers on strongly upright stems rarely need staking. 'Omega Skyrocket' is also sturdy and upright with pale blue flowers. 'Silver Moon' has white flowers. 'Blue Danube' has lavender-blue flowers 4 in. wide.

Symphyotrichum lateriflorum

calico aster

meadows

fall

2–3 × 2–3 ft.

part sun to sun

This perennial for full sun produces small leaves and petite, whitish pink flowers in profusion in early fall. It is not as large as other asters, but is a good species for its fine texture. It is still tough and drought resistant. The selection 'Lady in Black' is a superb cultivar producing a striking—but not flashy—specimen, broader than tall, with smoky green leaves, covering itself with ½ in. wide lavender-white flowers in late summer into autumn. 'Lovely' is also a top-notch cultivar, with dark green leaves. Heath aster (*Symphyotrichum ericoides*) has tiny leaves and small white flowers in excess. 'Snow Flurry' is a fine semievergreen cultivar of heath aster, creating a 1–2 in. tall ground cover or a cascade of growth over a wall.

Symphyotrichum oblongifolium*

aromatic aster

rock outcrops and dryish woods

fall

3–4 × 3–4 ft.

sun

Aromatic aster is one of the great fall asters, blooming late and long, and providing fragrance and attraction for fall pollinators for weeks. It is a sprawling, shrublike plant producing a myriad of showy, 1 in. wide flowers that are blue-violet with yellow centers. 'Raydon's Favorite' is a great cultivar, covering several square feet of space with a profusion of flowers. 'October Skies' is excellent, slightly smaller and tighter. These can be trained on a trellis, cut back by half in June, allowed to trail over a wall, or just left to ramble on a full-sun hillside. You will not be disappointed, and neither will the butterflies. A related species, smooth aster (*Symphyotrichum laeve*) is also worth growing. It is smaller, more delicate, and can take some shade. Try the cultivars 'Avondale', 'Photograph', and 'Bluebird'. On the other hand, the famous and widely sold New England and New York asters don't hold up well in our Southeast heat and humidity—grow them in the cooler mountains.

*syn. Aster oblongifolius

Thermopsis villosa

Carolina golden-banner

mountain woods openings

early summer

3–6 × 1–3 ft.

sun

This may be the closest you will get to easily growing a lupine in the warm Southeast—in fact, one common name is false-lupine. A strikingly handsome, tall plant, it makes a good garden specimen. However, because it grows wild only in the mountains, it will suffer from the lowland summer blues, and may need staking south of zone 7. Larry found it to bloom reliably for years in Charlotte, though it stretched in the warmth and needed sturdy staking.

Tradescantia ohiensis

smooth spiderwort

rich woods

spring, summer

1–2 × 1–2 ft.

part shade to part sun

Smooth spiderwort is an amazing plant. It grows elegantly erect, flowering day after day for weeks. The 1 in. wide flowers are showy, blue-lavender, with 3 rounded petals and unique, hairy yellow stamens (evident on all species of *Tradescantia*). Blooms open one per day from a tight, one-sided cluster of buds at the tip of the stem. Cut it back, and it will resprout, grow up, and keep on blooming. We believe the hairy stamens help bumblebees hold on for their rapid-fire visits. The "trads," as we call them, like to seed around the garden. Deadheading or cutting them completely down soon after the main show helps reduce the number of pop-up plants. 'Mrs. Loewer' has very narrow leaves and purple flowers; it needs full sun to grow well. Hairy spiderwort (*T. hirsuticaulis*), from rock outcrops, is 1 ft. tall, very compact, starts blooming in late winter and the whole plant disappears by summer. We love its abundant lavender-purple flowers.

Vernonia noveboracensis

ironweed

marshes and wet meadows

late summer

4–8 × 2–3 ft.

sun

Ironweed's huge clumps are glorious in bloom and attract wildlife, so plant them where the flowers can be seen. The blooms are showy, purple, and ½ in. long in large, loosely flat-topped clusters atop lush, leafy stems. They do become tall, but you can cut the stems back halfway by June 1 so they can branch and grow shorter before blooming; what you'll lose in architectural appeal you'll gain in access to the luscious flowers. Gray-leaved ironweed (*Vernonia glauca*) is a little smaller, with leaves that are more blue-green. Sandhills ironweed (*V. angustifolia*) grows only 4 ft. tall in drier conditions, with very narrow leaves. A recent favorite is *V. lettermannii* 'Iron Butterfly', a remarkable selection with abundant pink-purple flowers that insects love. With a meshwork of extremely thin, fine foliage that forms a well-branched, vigorous, sun-loving (or light shade) plant, 'Iron Butterfly' is also heat and drought tolerant.

Veronicastrum virginicum

Culver's root

moist to dry meadows, prairies

summer

3–6 × 2–3 ft.

part sun to sun

Culver's root first gained attention—as so many garden plants did—as a medicinal plant in the 17th century. It is stunning in a prairie situation, where stiffly erect grasses and broad-leaved plants dominate. It is not a dense plant, but has interesting narrow leaves produced in whorls along the gently branching stems. Erect inflorescences top the plant like candelabras, producing an abundance of small white flowers close on the stems. Site it in well-drained, loamy soil; it may become a bit overgrown in shade with too much water. It displays a unique growth form that brings an elegance to the garden, even though its presence is not overbearing.

Zizia aurea

golden Alexander

moist meadows and woods

spring, summer, fall, winter

1–3 × 1–3 ft.

part shade to sun

Because its flowers are individually small, golden Alexander needs to be planted in groups to draw your attention. Once established, it will form a colony from its fleshy taproots and may spread by seeds. The evergreen leaves are a joy in winter. The tiny yellow (sometimes maroon) flowers are delightful in their flat-topped clusters (umbels) on tall stems. The foliage has a distinctive odor that smells like parsley, and golden Alexanders serve as a most valuable larval food plant for black swallowtail butterflies. We would grow it just for the novelty of having a native member of the carrot family that is not Queen Anne's lace.

Vines

In growing vines for ornament, you'll need to provide two things: plenty of sunlight (for most) and a sturdy support. Give them an arbor, a fence, or a post, and they will create a crown of growth you can enjoy. They can be cut back hard periodically, or even every year, to the older woody branches. That forces them to grow out profusely in the spring with a new set of young stems bearing flowers, foliage, and eventually fruits. Be careful to not prune off spring flower buds or fruit-producing stems. Vines may climb by tendrils, clinging roots, or twining stems. The latter can strangle host plants, a good reason to keep them on a separate structure such as an arbor or trellis. Most are fast growing. Many have showy flowers or interesting seed pods, with a profusion of leaves that can create screening or hide an unsightly fence or arbor.

Ampelaster carolinianus*

climbing aster

swamps

late fall

4–10 ft.

part sun to sun

This wetland denizen of the Gulf Coast blooms heavily very late in the season, sometime surviving light frosts. It has a habit of sprawling and climbing without means of attachment, requiring support, but it is worth the effort. Without support, it just piles upon itself. Grow it on a fence or trellis, or, as is often done, let it grow up through a shrub and express itself outwardly from the shrub's branches. Its large, 1–2 in. wide pink flowers will appear as if out of nowhere. Climbing aster prefers moist soil, but is adaptable—the more moisture, the more flowers. You will come to anticipate—and enjoy—its late appearance to the show. Prune in late winter.

*syn. Aster carolinianus, Symphyotrichum carolinianum

*Aristolochia macrophylla**

Dutchman's pipevine

rich mountain forests

spring, summer, fall

8–20+ ft.

part shade to part sun

This pipevine is a very robust, fast-growing, high-climbing, deciduous, woody vine, ascending by twining stems. The large, heart-shaped, deciduous leaves can be a striking 12 in. wide, with weak yellow fall color. The peculiar S-curved flowers are often hidden under the newly developing leaves, but are worth a look. The hanging seed pods are fun to find; they split open to shake out flat seeds stacked inside like Pringles potato chips—fun for young gardeners. The foliage makes a wonderful mass to cover a porch, wall trellis, or arbor, as the tough stems weave their way through the slats—don't let it get into a tree or it will climb for the sky. Prune it in spring after flowering if needed, then let it regrow. This is a vital host plant for the pipevine swallowtail butterfly's distinctive red-maroon caterpillars. The protuding, hornlike appendages of these caterpillars may look alarming, but the insects are not at all dangerous.

*syn. *A. durior, Isotrema macrophylla*

Dutchman's pipevine leaf

◀ Dutchman's pipevine flower

*Bignonia capreolata**

cross-vine

low woods, swamps, roadsides

spring, simmer, fall, winter

5–20+ ft.

part sun to sun

This is a vigorous, semievergreen, woody vine that climbs by hooked leaf tendrils. Its common name refers to the brown "×" pattern inside the stem cut lengthwise at the node. Clusters of 2 in. long, tubular, red-orange-yellow flowers appear in midspring. These masses of gorgeous flowers are captivating, even if relatively brief. The beautiful fall and winter leaf color is a bonus. Popular cultivar 'Dragon Lady' has dark, ruby red, flaring flowers. 'Tangerine Beauty' has reddish orange flowers. Hummingbirds love the blooms. Prune the vine immediately after flowering and watch for basal runner vines that will strike out across the yard. As with other vines, best grown on a wooded post or arbor where it can cling and form a large mass without climbing high.

*syn. *Anisostichus capreolata*

Campis radicans

trumpet creeper

edges of woods and fence rows

summer, fall

5–20+ ft.

part sun to sun

Trumpet creeper is a long-blooming beauty that attracts hummingbirds all summer with its in-your-face flowers. The plant occupies much 3-dimensional space as its flexuous branches can extend several feet out from the main host trunk if left unpruned. It climbs the sides of trees using tenaciously clinging roots—so keep it off any tree trunk, pole, post, wall, or structure you want to protect. It needs a very sturdy support, and makes a great summertime screen with its coarsely divided leaves. Several color forms and hybrids are available, with striking bright flowers. While wonderful for hummingbirds, this unkempt, coarse vine is characteristic of pastureland fence posts throughout the Southeast, so tame it with caution—it can take over your house. Prune it just after flowering in summer if you have too much, or late winter.

Clematis viorna

northern leatherflower

ditch banks and thickets, low woods

summer, fall

6–10 ft.

part sun to sun

These captivating flowers are unbelievable: thick textured and so attractive that you want to go up and examine them—they're like pieces of hard candy. The fluffy seed heads may be even more exciting. The plant is informal in growth, forming sprawling tangles of small leaves and stems that are difficult to train. It can bloom all summer. Prune in late winter. Marsh clematis (*Clematis crispa*), also known as Southern leatherflower, is a widespread southeastern herbaceous species whose pink-blue-lavender flowers are much more open A very common clematis in the southern mountains is Virgin's-bower (*C. virginiana*), a sprawling, deciduous, woody vine that scrambles over other vegetation. The showy white flowers present in clusters scattered along the stems, making an inviting mantle en masse in late summer—a sure sign of the season. Fruit are a cluster of dry, plumose seeds that are scattered by the wind and most romantic when viewed with backlighting.

Decumaria barbara

climbing hydrangea

swamp forests and bottomlands

spring, summer, fall

5–20+ ft.

part shade to part sun

We love this vine; it has subtle details in all of its structures that are worthy of examination. It climbs effectively by its clinging roots, up tree trunks or on wooden fences. It has broad, unlobed, somewhat fleshy, shiny green leaves. It is quite attractive on a small limbed-up tree (say, a dogwood to 20 ft.) where it clothes the trunk in twiggy vines, handsome leaves with yellow fall color, and clusters of elegant white, fluffy flowers suddenly all in bloom for a week in midspring. It's even better on a fence, trellis, or arbor, so you can see and enjoy the flowers—otherwise, they're found mostly in treetops. This vine is very well behaved, except for the constant onslaught of vigorous basal vine-line offshoots crawling along the ground in search of another tree to climb. Prune them off, or watch out—they will pop up in some distant corner of the garden. Prune the upper branches immediately after flowering.

Gelsemium sempervirens

yellow jessamine

low woods and dry sandy hills

spring, summer, fall, winter

5–20+ ft.

part sun to sun

Yellow jessamine is one of the great southern vines: easy to grow, with evergreen foliage that is not too dense or coarse, and with abundant, fragrant, lemon-yellow flowers in very early spring. The thin, twining vine can climb, crawl, entangle, invade, mound, hang, strangle, wrap, and otherwise engulf almost anything—and it still looks great. It is captivating on a simple fan-shaped trellis in semi shade, where a see-through mass of judiciously trimmed, leafy growth is evenly covered with yellow flowers. It *will* find its way into your attic if you let it climb over the house, and it will self-sow in a garden situation. Find a way to use it somewhere anyway. It is charming and so indicative of the South (zone 8 and warmer)—and you can prune it back hard to keep it in bounds.

Lonicera sempervirens

coral honeysuckle

woods and thickets

spring, summer, fall, winter

6–10 ft.

part shade to sun

Coral honeysuckle is one of the most entertaining native plants of the Southeast. The long, woody, semi-evergreen vines twine rapidly and searchingly, as if eager to find their support and clamber up or over. If you try to move the vines to grow in one direction, they will spring back, as if to defy your suggestion. They are quintessential hummingbird flowers because of their bright red and yellow, tubular flowers. If the blooms are pollinated, red berries will be produced that can last into winter. When not in bloom, coral honeysuckle can be distinguished from the ubiquitous invasive Japanese honeysuckle (*Lonicera japonica*) by the latter's hairy stems and often lobed leaves that are not whitish underneath. 'Cedar Lane' is a profuse bloomer, 'John Clayton' has orange-yellow flowers, and 'Major Wheeler' blooms all summer, as does the thicker textured 'Alabama Crimson'. Prune immediately after flowering for rejuvenation. Be sure to get an ever-blooming selection.

Muscadinia rotundifolia*

muscadine

upland forests, swamps, thickets

spring, summer fall

5–20+ ft.

part sun to sun

Muscadine is one of the most ubiquitous grapes, both wild and cultivated, in the Southeast. There are many cultivar selections of muscadine (purple) and scuppernong (white) grapes; we rarely eat any of the other wild grapes. You would grow muscadine on a sturdy trellis or fence for its delectable fall fruit, but then you'd also notice the foliage turns a handsome autumn yellow and can be quite attractive. The tough, woody vines can smother small trees and shrubs that the vines grow on in full sun along roadsides—the same can happen in the garden if it gets away from you. Prune it in late winter on a very cold day well before new growth begins or it will harmlessly "bleed" sap.

*syn. Vitis rotundifolia

Passiflora incarnata

maypops

fencerows, fields, roadsides, and thickets

summer

3–10 ft.

sun

Everyone agrees that maypops, or passionflower, produces one of our most interesting and puzzling flowers, with its colorful petals and countless squiggly filaments. The foliage of this vigorous herbaceous perennial vine is clean and handsome in spring. It clambers and climbs via its grapevine-like tendrils. The complex and beautiful flowers are pink and blue and last only one day each, then develop into the familiar green, egg-sized fruit that pop! when you stomp them. Because it spreads aggressively from its extensive underground root system, it can be useful in a naturalized or managed meadow situation, but is not so easily maintained in the garden. Maybe grow it in a very large pot. It also looks tattered as summer progresses unless pruned back and watered to encourage resprouting. Most important, it is the exclusive larval host plant for several showy butterflies, including Gulf fritillary. Prune anytime to keep it in check. It resprouts from roots in the spring.

Smilax smallii

Jackson vine

coastal swamp forests

spring, summer, fall, winter

5–20+ ft.

shade to part sun

Normally we would not recommend a woody smilax, or catbrier, vine because the species are difficult to manage, impossible to eradicate, and viciously prickly. However, this famous species has been used widely throughout the Southeast as an attractive evergreen screening, fence adornment, and cover for house eaves. It is also cut judiciously and used in flower arrangements. It has minimal spines on the upper branches that bear the leaves. If you start with a young plant from tuberous roots, and keep it trained growing horizontally, it can be unmatched in foliar beauty. If, however, you let it climb high into a tree and make flowers and fruit (which is its inclination; the flowers are inconsequential ornamentally), the countless seeds will rain down upon the garden and grow wild into a jungle of unwieldly vines. Prune foliage anytime, and remove old stems as they die. Do not cut the main living stems.

Wisteria frutescens

American wisteria

low woods, streambanks, and moist meadows

spring, summer, fall

5–20+ ft.

part sun to sun

Our native wisteria is a delightful blue-flowering woody vine, certainly much tamer than the invasive Chinese and Japanese species that are known to strangle trees (and whole forests) to death. American wisteria differs from its Asian counterparts in its smaller leaves; shorter, denser, non-hanging flower clusters; and less fragrant flowers. It is a stout twiner with tough, woody stems—give it a sturdy trellis or arbor. Three good cultivars are 'Amethyst Falls', with blue flowers; 'Longwood Purple', with purple flowers; and 'Alba', with white flowers. Prune in late winter.

Shrubs

Shrubs are not just small trees; they are generally defined as woody plants that are multitrunked and less than 20 ft. tall, whereas trees grow taller and are generally single trunked. In nature, the diversity of shrubs is generally greater than that of trees. Shrubs provide cover and transition between forested and open habitats, where birds and small mammals can move between different types of plants to find food and cover. Because shrubs fill many niches in nature, they are invaluable in the garden. They are visible at eye level and can be used as foundation plantings near the home. Evergreens can help define space for privacy screening, while deciduous species can act as accent plants of striking beauty in flower and fruit. Shrubs bloom on either old growth from the previous year, or on new growth produced in the current year. If you prune before they bloom, you may be removing flower buds, so always plan to prune soon after flowering.

Aesculus parviflora

bottlebrush buckeye

rich woods

spring, summer, fall, winter

8–10 × 8–10 ft.

part shade to part sun

Bottlebrush buckeye is a first-rate garden plant, with four seasons of interest. The winter twigs have conspicuous buds. The 1–2 ft. plumes of white flowers are stunning in late spring to early summer, and a mature specimen puts on quite a show. The deciduous green leaves are bold and interesting, and their bright yellow fall color is exceptional. In early fall, large, ornamental, nutlike seeds are produced. The seeds are generally just smaller than golf balls, and look like beautifully polished wood spheres that have fallen on the ground. Pick them up for display in a bowl. They shrivel as soon as they dry, and must be planted immediately if you want to grow them. In the warmer zones of the Southeast, it should not have direct afternoon sun, so plant bottlebrush buckeye in very light open shade or on the sunny edge of a woodland border where it will get strong morning sun.

Aesculus pavia

red buckeye

moist woods

spring, fall

5–10 × 3–8 ft.

part shade to part sun

Red buckeye is one of our best native shrubs. It is unique for its striking, early-spring, bright red tubular flowers that greet the early migrating hummingbirds. It grows slowly, but it is long lived. Try to find a place for one somewhere in the garden; its spring growth is fascinating to watch as the husky new stem, big leaves, and large flowering cluster emerge from a single tip bud. In late summer, round, light brown seeds drop from their leathery pods and look like polished wood on the ground. Pick them up for display and good luck. Fall color is lacking. Ohio buckeye (*Aesculus glabra*) is larger and coarser; it has pale yellow flowers and not much ornamental value.

*Agarista populifolia**

Florida hobblebush

swamps

spring, summer, fall, winter

8–12 × 8–12 ft.

shade to part sun

Even though the abundant flowers are of little visual consequence—white, tubular, ½ in. long, fragrant, and inconspicuous in clusters under the foliage—this is one of the very best shade-loving evergreen shrubs for privacy screening, garden backgrounds, or streambanks. It makes a very large, loose clump with long, upward-and-outward arching stems that will benefit from periodic thinning. Children can make a tunnel or cave within its undergrowth. The glossy dark-green foliage looks good all year round, and is clean and free of disease. Do not grow in full sun or where the soil dries out. It can tolerate very wet soils. If cut to the ground, it rejuvenates quickly. A dwarf cultivar named Leprechaun™, growing about 5 × 4 ft., is an excellent garden plant.

*syn. *Leucothoe populifolia*

Amelanchier arborea

downy serviceberry

forests

spring, summer, fall, winter

10–20 × 10–15 ft.

part sun to sun

In earlier times, serviceberry's early masses of white flowers were a harbinger of spring throughout the southern Appalachian Mountains, signaling the opportunity to have a religious "service" (wedding or funeral) after a cold, snowy winter during which roads were impassable. It can be considered a small tree or large shrub; either way it is one of the best plants, with fabulous traits—flowers, foliage, fruit, fall color, and bark—that are above average, making this a five-star choice. An excellent selection is 'Autumn Brilliance', which is a large, twiggy shrub. This selection has excellent fall color and disease resistance and does not get very large. Other similar outstanding selections are 'Princess Diana' and 'Autumn Sunset'. As they mature, they can produce juicy, tasty, red-purple berries in early summer, and are good for humans if you can get them before the birds. Any of these would be first-rate specimen garden plants.

Aronia arbutifolia

red chokeberry

low woods and swamps

spring, fall, winter

5–10 × 3–5 ft.

part sun to sun

Red chokeberry is a fabulous semievergreen shrub, especially if you like red. It grows fast and lush, forms loose colonies, and adapts well to average or wet soil and light shade or sun (though you get a lot more berries in the sun). The white flowers are nice in spring, but the prolific fall berries are striking red and last through the cold of winter. The fall color is a brilliant shade of scarlet. An excellent cultivar is 'Brilliantissima', producing slightly larger red berries and glaringly scarlet-red fall leaf color on a more compact plant. Black chokeberry (*Aronia melanocarpa*) is similar except that its juicy, ⅜ in. wide berries are purple-black. Its berries look good up close, but may not show up as well in the garden. It does have excellent fall color, though, and is widely available in various landscape sizes.

Callicarpa americana

beautyberry

rocky woods and thickets

summer, fall

6–10 × 4–8 ft.

part shade to sun

The main reason to grow this ungainly shrub is for the extraordinary show of gaudy purple, ¼ in. wide berries in late summer and early autumn, persisting until birds eat them all, which is usually very quickly. It will soon grow into an unmanageable thicket, and should periodically be cut back hard—even to the ground, even every winter. It will flower and make fruit on new growth the same year. The berries drop off readily when branches are cut, so avoid bringing beautyberry inside. It self-sows readily, and excess seedlings should be removed from the garden. The numerous small pink flowers are produced in summer, clustered around each leaf pair, and are not especially attractive, except to bees. Despite these issues, it is always a treat to see the colorful berries and watch the birds go bonkers over them—especially in someone else's yard! An elegant, heavy fruited, white-berried form (variety *lactea*) is also available.

Calycanthus floridus

sweet-shrub

woods and streambanks

spring, fall

4–8 × 4–8 ft.

shade to part sun

This is one of the most widely recognized shrubs in the Southeast, often affectionately known as "bubbie bush," perhaps because in earlier times, rural ladies would place one of the spicy scented flowers in their bosoms as perfume. Scratching the twigs also releases the wonderful scent. On fall woodland walks, show children the 3 in. long, fat, papery seed pods and point out that they must be chewed open by mice to get the seeds as food. It is usually seen as an informal, slow-spreading shrub. The cultivar 'Athens' has attractive, greenish yellow spring flowers with intense fragrance. There is some confusion about the flowers' scent—it is produced only on the first day the flower opens, and then only in the evening 2 hr. before dark, to attract tiny pollinating beetles. The flower then closes (trapping the beetles for pollination), to open again the next day—odorless. Many gardeners look forward to this enjoyable monthlong aromatic experience each spring.

Cephalanthus occidentalis

buttonbush

swamps and marshes	
summer, fall	
6–8 × 6–8 ft.	
part sun to sun	

Buttonbush is a big green shrub, but the curious 2 in. wide flower spheres, with flower styles sticking out like a pincushion, are amazing butterfly magnets. You will love the display in midsummer—a time when few other shrubs bloom. In the fall, the fruiting balls turn red, fall apart, and provide food for waterfowl. In a larger landscape, or near a pond or lake, buttonbush can actually grow in up to 3 ft. of standing water, and it is worth the space. It can be cut to the ground to rejuvenate when it becomes overgrown. It also has a decent fall color show when it is grown in sun.

Clethra alnifolia

coastal sweet-pepperbush

moist pine woods and shrubby wetlands

summer, fall

2–6 × 2–4 ft.

part sun to sun

You do not want to be without coastal sweet-pepperbush, often called summersweet, in your garden. The sweet fragrance is glorious, and the flowers readily attract butterflies. The upright growth, bright white flower spikes, and handsome, dark green summer foliage make for multiple pleasing features. It does not spread rapidly, but does creep underground through the shrub border, though is quite manageable. Coastal sweet-pepperbush is often used to fill in space in medians and beds, and offers nice yellow color in fall. *Clethra alnifolia* is especially nice in its pink forms, the brightest being 'Ruby Spice'—highly recommended if you have room for only one form. Mountain sweet-pepperbush (*C. acuminata*) gets taller, 8–15 ft., and has beautiful mahogany peeling bark. The mountain form likes cooler climes (zones 6–7), and may be shy to grow well in the warmer parts of the Southeast.

Croton alabamensis

Alabama croton

rocky woods and glades

spring, summer, fall, winter

6–10 × 5–8 ft.

part shade to part sun

This shrub is a gem for the garden, and a little bit different than ordinary plants. Its 2–5 in. long apple-green leaves turn a bright orange color in late autumn and are covered underneath with silvery scales. A few of the leaves stay on as silvery ornaments through winter, and the clusters of winter buds open to reveal small bright yellow flowers in late winter. The ½ in. long gray seed pods are subtle, but evident in summer. It can be left alone, or pruned informally. It comes exclusively from central Alabama, but every serious gardener should have one.

Alabama croton leaves

Alabama croton bloom

Cyrilla racemiflora

swamp titi

wet coastal shrub lands

spring, summer, fall, winter

6–15 × 10–15 ft.

part sun to sun

Swamp titi is a whimsical semievergreen shrub that grows informally into a large shrub—give it room. About half of the handsome 2–3 in. long leathery green leaves turn rusty red-yellow before falling. In early summer, numerous 4 in. tall spikes of small white flowers appear in pendulous clusters that attract the most unusual array of colorful insects you ever saw. In winter, it features attractive brown bark with low ridges. It actually makes an interesting informal foundation plant for places where you can prune it to fit the space without ruining its effect. Bees make honey from the nectar.

Diervilla sessilifolia

southern bush-honeysuckle

mountain openings and streambanks

spring, summer, fall

3–5 × 2–4 ft.

part sun to sun

While at its best in the mountains, bush-honeysuckle can be tried in warmer areas. It makes a surprisingly neat and tidy shrub with little pruning, and the long-blooming, informal yellow flowers are delightful. The fall color is reddish purple. It is often used as a small foundation or border shrub. Cultivar 'Copper' is a handsome, dwarf selection with dark leaves.

Dirca palustris

leatherwood

rich woods

spring, summer, fall, winter

3–8 × 3–4 ft.

shade to part sun

This is Larry's favorite shrub. It is not showy, ever, but its charm will win you over in subtle ways. It is rare throughout eastern America. We like the unusual early-spring flowers, tiny though they are, and the delicate frill around the new leaves. The mature leaves seem indistinctive, but their shape is unique, subtly angled yet rounded. The little greenish fruit come and go without much notice—they can form a colony of plants around the mother. The form of the shrub is usually upright and formal. The fall color is a nice yellow. The twigs are unusually jointed and very flexible, and were purportedly used as ties and thongs by indigenous peoples. In fact, they can be tied into knots right on the plant, where they will grow that way for years.

Euonymus americanus

American strawberry-bush

dryish woods

fall, winter

4–8 × 3–4 ft.

part shade to part sun

This is a well-known and adaptable species that has a place in every woodland garden. There is no more wonderful sight in the fall to show people, especially children, than the 1 in. wide bright red pods splitting open to reveal the attractive orange seeds of American strawberry-bush, or hearts-a-burstin'—a wonderful alternative common name. The seeds are relished by birds. The ½ in. wide spring flowers are insignificant. It is a popular plant among those establishing a native woodland garden because it is so easy to grow and provides attractive green stems for winter interest. Just plant it and forget it—until fall. Then you can say, "Wow! Come look at this!"

Fothergilla gardenii

dwarf fothergilla

moist, open pinewoods

spring, summer, fall, winter

2–4 × 3–5 ft.

part sun to sun

This is one of our most appealing shrubs, with year-round interest. It slowly spreads to create an informal mass. The white, compact, bottle-brush flowers in early spring are delicate and delightful, the summer foliage is handsome, and the fall color is spectacular, especially when grown in sun. The plants are neat, upright, and adaptable. They mix well with other deciduous shrubs and rarely become too large. Plant several in your garden for viewing from different vantage points. The cultivar 'Blue Mist' has handsome, blue-green foliage in summer, but are not as reliable for good fall color. 'Mount Airy' is a hybrid with the rare large fothergilla (*Fothergilla major*). It is widely available and vigorous, growing to 8 ft. or taller (it can be cut back hard), featuring large flower clusters and leaves, and producing consistently good fall color. Very highly recommended.

Hydrangea quercifolia

oakleaf hydrangea

wooded ravines

spring, summer, fall, winter

4–10 × 4–10 ft.

part shade to part sun

This is one of the great plants of the Southeast, but very large and coarse and therefore difficult to use in a small landscape. It is tolerant of heat, cold, and drought, and can take full sun (but doesn't like it). The very large ½–1 ft. long clusters of white flowers are a mixture of smaller normal and showy sterile, that dry nicely in the winter. If the plant becomes too large, simply cut back—even to the ground—and it will resprout. Its spectacular floral display and unmatched fall colors of red, yellow, and rich purple make it an excellent garden choice. The winter stems are interesting, with flaking bark and large tip buds. Cultivar 'Alice' is strikingly floriferous and robust, becoming 12 ft. tall and wide; Snow Queen™ is large, with many double flowers. 'Peewee' is a 5 ft. dwarf. 'Munchkin' grows to only 2–3 ft.

Hydrangea radiata

silverleaf hydrangea

rich mountain forests and roadsides

spring, summer

3–8 × 3–8 ft.

part shade to part sun

Silverleaf hydrangea is a wonderful shrub, blooming well in summer shade when little else is in flower in the woods. The tiny white flowers are aggregated into large, flat-topped clusters 3–6 in. wide, with 5–15 sterile flowers around the margin, making it attractive as a native "lace-cap" in the semiformal shrub border. The peely brownish bark is attractive in winter. The white undersides of the leaves are striking when the wind flutters them over. It can be thinned out annually for a neater look, or cut back heavily if it becomes too overgrown. Be aware that it blooms only on new growth that comes from the previous year's woody stem, so don't cut every stem completely to the ground. Grows beautifully well beyond the mountains. More widespread throughout the Southeast is smooth hydrangea (*Hydrangea arborescens*). Heat and drought tolerant, it is similar to the silverleaf, except the leaves are green underneath and the plant produces fewer sterile flowers. Popular cultivar 'Annabelle' has abundant white mophead flower clusters.

Hypericum frondosum

shrubby St. John's wort

open moist areas

spring, summer, fall, winter

3–4 × 3–4 ft.

sun

The shrubby St. John's worts are widely used because they are sun loving, compact, long flowering, and adaptable to a wide range of conditions. *Hypericum frondosum* 'Sunburst' is a widely grown cultivar, reaching 4 ft. tall. It has narrow, bluish green leaves (a few may remain through mild winters), and very large, yellow, powder-puff flowers. It is excellent in full-sun rain gardens. *Hypericum prolificum* is particularly floriferous and compact, with ½ in. wide, bright yellow flowers appearing as a puffy ball of yellow stamens, offering a diversion from the all-green foundation shrubs we usually see. Other species of interest are *H. tenuifolium* (syn. *H. reductum*) and *H. lloydii*, which have small, needlelike leaves to 1 in. long and make dense, clumping shrublets that are useful in dryish rock gardens and well-drained sunny sites. *Hypericum densiflorum* is a taller shrub (2–4 ft.), with attractive, ½ in. wide, yellow flowers, flaking bark, and narrow leaves.

Ilex glabra

inkberry holly

moist pine forests and peatlands

spring, summer, fall, winter

4–8 × 2–3 ft.

part sun to sun

Inkberry holly, also known as little gallberry, is not a flashy plant, but is a good evergreen species for foundations and other situations where you want something green all year round that you don't have to prune (much). The small white flowers and even the ¼ in. wide black berries are not very showy, and like most hollies, the birds don't eat them until they have to, in late winter. There are several cultivars available; 'Shamrock' is favored for its shiny dark green leaves. Most hollies are reported to be at least somewhat deer resistant. These useful shrubs spread very slowly, and the cultivars seem to not spread at all.

Ilex verticillata

winterberry

swamps and shrubby wetlands

fall, winter

6–8 × 4–8 ft.

part sun to sun

This deciduous holly is one of the best shrubs for winter color, because the bright red, ¼ in. wide berries are visible and persistent. They are not highly nutritious to birds, so are eaten later in winter as emergency food. A flock of cedar waxwings, robins, or cardinals can wipe them out quickly, though. Because the male and female flowers of all hollies are on separate plants—one of nature's little tricks—you need to plant two compatible selections nearby. Herein lies a quandary. Different male and female selections (from different parts of the country) bloom at slightly different times. You must match your two to have a compatible pair. So, the female selection 'Winter Red' (one of the most widely planted), requires cultivar 'Southern Gentleman' as a pollinator because they both bloom late. But the larger-berried 'Red Sprite' is happy with the earlier blooming 'Jim Dandy'. You only need one male for 6 (or so) females.

Ilex vomitoria

yaupon holly

coastal forests

spring, summer, fall, winter

6–20 × 4–10 ft.

part sun to sun

Normal-sized yaupon holly (versus the dwarf selection 'Nana' that follows) is a dense, upright shrub with dark, evergreen foliage. It makes an excellent landscape specimen for foundations or screening, is very attractive in winter, and has persistent red berries with green leaves. It is not reliably hardy if exposed to prolonged temperatures below 0°F. Typically you would let it grow to about 10 ft., but it can get up to 20 ft. over time, so can make a tall screening hedge. Cut it back hard as necessary. A striking weeping cultivar, 'Pendula', grows to 15 ft. and is loaded with berries if you have a male plant nearby (like all hollies). Tall males generally do not have cultivar names (but tall 'Will Fleming' and dwarf 'Schillings' might work for you), so look for the plants without berries in a group of berried selections in autumn at the nursery. Female cultivars include 'Yawkey', with yellow berries. 'Carolina Ruby' berries are candy-apple red and 'Virginia Dare' berries are orange.

Ilex vomitoria 'Nana'

dwarf yaupon holly

dry, sandy woods

spring, summer, fall, winter

1–4 × 1–4 ft.

part sun to sun

This is a landscape staple as a low-growing, tough, never-needs-pruning foundation and border plant. It is a great selection: heat and drought tolerant, very dense and slow growing (to perhaps 3–4 ft. tall in 15 years, in moist conditions), and it regrows well when damaged or cut back. There is no finer native evergreen dwarf plant—it looks like a dwarf boxwood. But, it never does anything. No flowers, no berries, no perceptible change. That's fine. Plant it anyway! There are several other selections of dwarf yaupon available. One with really tiny leaves that has done well is 'Micron', and slightly larger is 'Schillings', which can act as a male pollinator for berried types. The "wild type" yaupon holly grows as an informal shrub, 10 × 10 ft. or more, can be pruned, and has beautiful foliage for foundations or screening. It can make abundant red berries if male and female specimens are present.

Illicium floridanum

Florida anisetree

woods and swamps

spring, summer, fall, winter

6–12 × 6–8 ft.

part shade to part sun

In its best form, this plant resembles a broad-leaved rhododendron (the red leaf stalks add a touch of distinction), and it may fill that textural niche as southeastern summers become warmer and drier. The strong anise scent from the crushed foliage is unpleasant to some (especially deer), acceptable to others. The unusual flowers are a pleasant maroon with many radiating, narrow petals, resembling a flattened octopus. Exceptional as an adaptable, heat- and drought-tolerant, shade-loving, cold-adaptive, broad-leaved native evergreen. In sun, the leaves will yellow and scorch. It can be sheared, pruned, thinned, cut back, and otherwise manipulated—or just left alone for years—and it will still grow back rapidly. Give it some room (6–8 ft. wide) and let it flourish. There are several selections; all are good. Our favorite is 'Halley's Comet', which reblooms almost continuously. 'Pink Frost' is light green and variegated. We find these selections outstanding—and we like the scent!

Illicium parviflorum

yellow anisetree

swamps and forests in Florida

spring, summer, fall, winter

6–10 × 6–10 ft.

part sun to sun

Illicium parviflorum has been used for years as a heat-tolerant, tough evergreen for light shade and sun. The flowers are small, yellowish, and inconspicuous; the leaves are light green. It spreads slowly by suckering or layering, and gets to about 8–10 ft. tall and wide. It makes a great plant for a forgotten back corner, or as a see-through, never-prune living hedge between properties. Its light anise scent has both fans and detractors. The cultivar 'Forest Green' has darker leaves; 'Florida Sunshine' is a compact shrub with brilliant yellow foliage that looks great in the winter garden (keep from hot sun and drying). Yellow anisetree is a tough, useful plant, especially for foundations and screening in the warm South. Probably not reliably hardy below 10°F.

Itea virginica

Virginia-willow

swamps and wetlands

spring, fall

3–5 × 3–8 ft., spreading

part shade to sun

Virginia-willow (not a true willow), perhaps better known as Virginia sweetspire, produces a wonderful informal, semievergreen, spreading colony that would need to be managed to keep within bounds—but it works well with other shrubs in an informal border or grouping. The white, late-spring flowers are fragrant on arching, graceful stalks, attracting butterflies. The fall colors can be uniformly red-purple or a mixture, depending on sun exposure (more sun, more purple). It can grow well in difficult situations, such as wet areas, moderate shade, and uneven terrain such as a ravine, ditch, or rain garden. Its only fault is that it spreads, but it is still not overpoweringly aggressive. One of the best selections is 'Henry's Garnet', with consistent reddish purple fall color. Smaller forms are Little Henry™ and 'Merlot'; both are dwarf and compact (to 3 ft.). More upright and with good yellow-orange-red fall color in cooler zone 7 is 'Saturnalia'.

Kalmia latifolia

mountain laurel

dryish forests, bluffs, and streambanks

spring, summer, fall, winter

3–8 × 3–5 ft.

part shade to part sun

Mountain laurel is a beautiful and well-known evergreen shrub made famous by 18th-century plant collectors. It is ubiquitous in dry, rocky forests and exposed road banks in the mountains. As a young specimen, it makes a symmetrical green bush covered in flower clusters. The flowers are beautiful, providing the unique experience of watching each stamen (there are ten) spring up and throw its pollen when triggered by a visiting bee. It does not grow in clay soils, and must have perfect drainage and even moisture until well established. Planting in a loamy soil with leaf compost, perhaps in a raised bed, is ideal. Older, leggy, or broken plants can be rejuvenated if pruned to near the ground just after spring bloom. Many cultivars are available. If you want to grow it in a warmer region, obtain one from a nursery that grew it from seeds of that region.

Leucothoe axillaris

coastal doghobble

swamps and thickets

spring, summer, fall, winter

2–3 × 3–4 ft.

shade to part sun

This evergreen mounding shrub grows wider than tall, with dark green, pointy leaves on gracefully arching, zigzaggy stems that form a tangle (and can "hobble" hunting dogs). The attractive, tubular, white, late-spring flowers are numerous, hanging down on spikes partly hidden under the leaves. This handsome shrub is widely used as a thick-textured foundation or border plant—it can sucker to form a slowly enlarging mound. Coastal doghobble must be kept moist and does not like drying wind, but loves light shade or part sun. The most common problem is letting it dry out. A beautiful, disease-resistant cultivar is 'Margie Jenkins', with broader leaves that turn red-purple in fall. Mountain doghobble (*Leucothoe fontanesiana*) is the attractive highland cousin of the coastal species. The mountain plant is larger, it blooms in late spring in moist woods and road banks, and its flowers are a little larger and more conspicuous. It can hobble larger dogs.

Lindera benzoin

spicebush

rich woods and bottomland forests

spring, fall

6–10 × 5–10 ft.

shade to part sun

While it is a harbinger of earliest spring with its countless small, bright yellow flowers in clusters along the branches, spicebush's most attractive time is when the red fruit are ripening against yellow foliage in early autumn. The fruit are quickly consumed by birds. Try scratching and sniffing the twigs in winter for a spicy fragrance, and enjoy the conspicuous yellow-green buds that some folks steep into a tea. It is an open deciduous shrub that can harbor wildflowers beneath it. It is also a larval food source for spicebush swallowtail and eastern swallowtail butterflies. The sexes are on separate plants, so you will need male and female specimens growing together to get the red berries.

Lyonia lucida

shining fetterbush

swamps and shrubby peatlands

spring, summer, fall, winter

3–8 × 2–6 ft.

part sun to sun

This is a handsome evergreen shrub with an informal, upright-arching growth form that slowly becomes a larger clump. The charming little pink, urn-shaped flowers are produced in early spring, amidst the handsome, dark green leaves. It's a little different from most landscape plants, but we consider it one of the best evergreen native shrubs—whether the conditions are dry (but not too dry), wet, shady, or sunny. Folks in the Deep South are already familiar with it as a useful landscape plant in the heat and humidity.

*Morella cerifera**

common wax-myrtle

coastal moist and dry, sandy habitats

spring, summer, fall, winter

5–10 × 5–10 ft.

part sun to sun

Common wax-myrtle, sometimes called southern bayberry, has long been known as a source of fragrant candle wax, which is derived from its fruit. The plants grow variably, and can be dense and leafy or thin and semievergreen. They can also be clumping or suckering. Prune wax-myrtle anytime; it can be limbed up to expose the interesting bark on the trunks. In wind-swept, coastal situations, it makes a great beach-home landscape planting. Only the females will have the blue, waxy fruit, so males must be part of a mixed planting. Everything about this plant is excellent: the forms, the fragrant foliage, and the blue winter fruit (which birds will eat). It is best in full sun and well-drained soil. Keep it watered during droughts to reduce stress. Of great value in landscaping is dwarf wax-myrtle. It is smaller, to 4 ft., with smaller leaves, and tends to spread a bit more. One such excellent cultivar is 'Don's Dwarf'.

*syn. *Myrica cerifera*

Opuntia humifusa*

eastern prickly-pear cactus

sandy or rocky open habitats

spring, summer, fall, winter

6 in. × 1–3 ft.

part sun to sun

Now for something a little different in the garden. Did you realize cacti are woody shrubs? They have a hard internal skeleton, and their "branches" are green flattened pads. Prickly-pear cactus works well in a dry, open setting—probably best by itself on a rocky outcrop. The large yellow flowers are attractive, opening only in bright sunlight, blooming in early summer and sporadically later. Fruits are large, juicy, red berries with many black seeds. The pads stand out in winter, but be sure to grow it in a very well-drained site or it will rot in cold, wet situations. The large and smaller spines are barbed and can be very irritating. You do not want to grow this plant where you would accidentally touch it while weeding, or where a child might fall on or try to play with it. One source suggests this is the best cactus for green roofs in the Southeast.

*syn. *O. compressa*

Physocarpus opulifolius

ninebark

streambanks and thickets

spring, summer, fall, winter

3–9 × 3–9 ft.

part sun to sun

Ninebark gets its name from the plant's peeling and shredding bark, in "nine layers," which is striking in winter. It has a unique growth form, very broad and rounded, with numerous branches that gracefully weep nearly to the ground when open grown. In late spring, clusters of white, briefly showy flowers appear at the tips of the branches. The dry pod clusters are persistent but not particularly ornamental. Still, it is an interesting and worthwhile shrub—especially the cultivars—through the mountains and cooler Upper Southeast. A striking, black-purple, dark-leaved selection is Diablo®. Not likely to hold its dark color through hot summers outside the mountains, Diablo is still a nice shrub with striking white-flower/black-leaf contrast when in spring bloom. The leaves on Summer Wine® emerge red, then darken to purple. 'Dart's Gold' has bright yellow leaves.

Rhapidophyllum hystrix

needle palm

swampy woods

spring, summer, fall, winter

8–10 × 8–10 ft.

part shade to part sun

Palms are usually associated with the tropics, so here's your chance to create a tropical paradise in your more temperate backyard. They look great around a partly shaded swimming pool (in the ground or in very large pots) or as specimen plants in a spacious woodland garden. Needle palm is the most cold hardy of all palms, surviving below -10°F when established in the ground. The 5–8 ft. handlike leaves remain attractive all year, even holding up well with snow on the large leaves. The small tan flowers appear in grapelike clusters along the trunk. Avoid the sharp, 1 ft. "needles" that presumably protect the unripe seeds from wildlife. Widely available wherever palms are sold.

Rhododendron calendulaceum

flame azalea

mountain woods

spring, fall

6–10 × 4–8 ft.

part shade to part sun

Flame azalea is an iconic native of the high country, especially along the Blue Ridge Parkway. It is tall, with orange to yellow, non-fragrant flowers that bloom in early summer. While acceptable in the Piedmont of the Upper South, it prefers the cooler, wetter climate of the mountains. Similar in appearance, the Florida flame azalea (*Rhododendron austrinum*), also known as the Piedmont flame, blooms in early spring with orange to yellow, mildly fragrant flowers. It is a better flame azalea for the Piedmont and Deep South regions. Oconee azalea (*R. flammeum*, syn. *R. speciosum*) is a midspring bloomer with gorgeous red-orange-yellow, thick-textured flowers on slightly shorter plants. Oconee azalea is more heat tolerant than the classic mountain flame azalea. The plumleaf azalea (*R. prunifolium*) should be sought out, as its knockout red-orange flowers bloom in midsummer, despite the warmth, attracting butterflies and hummingbirds. Plumleaf is the slowest to reach flowering age, so buy the largest plant possible.

Rhododendron maximum

rose-bay rhododendron

mountain forests

spring, summer, fall, winter

8–12 × 5–10 ft.

part shade to part sun

This is an omnipresent, large evergreen shrub in the mountains, dominant in virtually every moist forest and shady roadside with acidic soil. It is beautiful in bloom, and provides the long-term midsummer displays of white to light pink, large-clustered flowers so characteristic along the Blue Ridge Parkway. It grows along streams and steep hillsides and usually forms dense, impenetrable "rhododendron hells." It is fast growing as a wild plant around mountain homes, to the point of becoming obstructing in some places. Just cut them down to near ground level; they will regrow readily. The Catawba or purple rhododendron (*Rhododendron catawbiense*) is a cold-hardy species forming vast stretches of early-summer bloom on open balds and roadsides in the southern Appalachian Mountains above 3000 ft. Neither of these beautiful wild plants is recommended for the garden outside the mountains (zones 6–7). The well-known lavender rhododendron widely grown in mountain home landscapes is the hybrid cultivar 'English Roseum'.

Rhododendron minus

dwarf rhododendron

mountain streambanks and rocky outcrops

spring, summer, fall, winter

4–10 × 3–6 ft.

shade to part sun

Dwarf rhododendron is a small-leaved rhododendron that makes an exceptional shrub for light shade or part sun. If you want to try an evergreen rhododendron outside the cool mountains, this is the one. It is one of our most beautiful species, growing into a handsome shrub with very splashy, white to deep pink flowers that are not particularly fragrant. It makes a stunning flower display in the shrub border or in an informal woodland setting. It is also easier to grow than the large-leaved rhododendrons—heat tolerant and more tolerant of various well-drained soils, but still needing mulch and regular watering. The deeper into the South you go, the more its performance is likely to disappoint, so check your local nurseries for proven selections. There are some beautiful hybrid cultivars, including 'Dora Amateis', 'Cornell Pink', 'Olga Mezitt', and 'Llenroc'. The 'PJM' hybrids have very good foliage, but tend to bloom out in the fall.

Rhododendron periclymenoides

pinxter azalea

woods and streambanks

spring, fall

6–10 × 4–6 ft.

part shade to part sun

There are no finer flowering shrubs than our native azaleas, often referred to as "deciduous azaleas," in contrast to the ubiquitous evergreen Japanese azalea hybrids used in home landscaping throughout the South. Our natives are easy-to-grow shrubs with striking flowers and good fall color; even in winter, the large, dormant flower buds have appeal. They are excellent for naturalizing in open woodland gardens or for massing in semi-sunny shrub borders. The quality of their environment in June, as they make their new buds, determines the quantity of flowers the following year—so water them during droughts and give them a half-day of sun if possible. Native azaleas prefer acidic soil. Their roots are shallow, so provide light mulch and adequate moisture. Pinxter azalea produces large clusters of 2–3 in. wide, tubular, light to dark pink, fragrant spring flowers with countless protruding stamens appealing to butterflies and clearwing moths. Closely related and often grown is Piedmont azalea (*Rhododendron canescens*).

Rhus aromatica

fragrant sumac

rocky wooded slopes

summer, fall, winter

1–5 × 2–5 ft.

part shade to sun

Fragrant sumac is a charming shrub that looks almost exactly like a diminutive poison oak in leaf, but is not poisonous (sumacs with red berries are never poisonous, only those with white fruit such as poison ivy, poison oak, and poison sumac). This is a creeping informal shrub, though it may form mounds in sunny sites and can be trained on a fence or trellis. The tiny yellow flowers bloom in late winter, and it produces small clusters of hairy red berries that birds will eat. Even in part sun, the fall color is outstanding; in winter it is fun to scratch the twigs and smell the spicy fragrance. It is very drought tolerant and a tough survivor. Cultivar 'Low Grow' forms a loose, open shrub to 8 ft. tall and as wide, but does not spread much; this shrub offers great fall color and is an excellent choice for a dry median, rocky bank, or shrub border.

Sambucus canadensis

elderberry

swamp forests, low woods, floodplains, pastures, ditches

spring, summer

8–10 × 8–10 ft.

part sun to sun

Elderberry is one of the most common and familiar shrubs in our region. It is a superstar for birds and insects. Humans use the flowers in fritters and salads, and the juicy, purple, ⅛ in. wide berries make wonderful wine, pies, and jams. Fresh and vibrant in spring, it produces blooms and fruit all summer. By early fall, though, the plants become more overgrown and worn, disheveled and unsightly. Elderberry can (and should) be cut back hard each year, but keep about 6 in. of woody stems near the base to regenerate the new shoots that will flower and fruit the following year. Cultivar 'Aurea' has red fruit and looks good all season. 'Maxima' has much larger flower clusters. Planting two different selections will allow for greater fruit production.

Vaccinium corymbosum

highbush blueberry

swamps, bogs, and wet woods

spring, summer, fall

4–8 × 4–10 ft.

part sun to sun

Who doesn't love blueberries? They are the quintessential wild, juicy berry that we know we can eat without consequence. Thanks to the many species, there is seemingly a blueberry for every size and habitat need. They are mostly deciduous (with 1–2 in. long leaves), have great multihued fall color, and adapt to hard pruning as landscape specimens. Bees and hummingbirds like the flowers, and birds like the fruit—so get up early to pick berries when they are ripe. Huckleberries appear similar, but have seedy fruit and prefer drier sites. Highbush blueberry gives us the tasty blueberry of commerce. Grow several cultivars for cross-pollination and have a beautiful edible landscape. Be sure the soil is kept acidic or the leaves will yellow and become chlorotic. They really should be grown in full sun to produce the most berries. Lowbush blueberries (*Vaccinium tenellum*, *V. vacillans*) are rhizomatous, spreading, dwarf deciduous shrubs to 2 ft. tall.

highbush blueberry fruit

highbush blueberry flower

Viburnum dentatum

arrowwood

dry woods, streambanks, floodplain forests

spring, summer, fall, winter

6–10 × 4–8 ft.

part sun to sun

Viburnums are staples of the shrub garden. This species is deciduous and clump forming. Its slender stems are often very straight, giving rise to the common name. The small, white flowers are in flat-topped clusters, producing dryish, blue-black berries. Viburnums are reported to have good fall color, but not all do. A good cultivar for color in southern gardens is 'Osceola'. A shorter selection (4–5 ft.) is Blue Muffin™, with striking, glossy green summer leaves and plentiful, porcelain-blue berries. Be sure to plant compatible male and female selections. The more sun, the better for viburnums. Maple-leaved viburnum (*Viburnum acerifolium*) is a short (4–5 ft.), spreading, deciduous shrub with 3-lobed leaves that look very much like red maple. This species turns a good rusty red in autumn, and has a few black berries; it is highly desirable because of its low stature and attractive foliage.

Viburnum nudum

smooth witherod

streambanks and wetlands

spring, summer, fall, winter

4–8 × 4–6 ft.

part sun to sun

Of all the viburnums, this clump-forming deciduous species is the most famous and ornamental. This is one beautiful shrub for its multicolored, berrylike fruit, often with 4 colors at the same time. The fruit are in clusters and turn from green to pink to red to blue over a long period. They mature in late summer, and are readily eaten by birds. The leaves then turn a rich red-purple in fall. It is a plant for all seasons, as its winter buds are large. Two good, widely available selections are 'Pink Beauty', with many fruit and stunning fall color; and 'Winterthur', one of the superstars with great fall leaves and colorful fruit that birds relish.

Viburnum obovatum

Walter's viburnum

thickets and swamp margins

spring, summer, fall, winter

2–10 × 2–8 ft.

part sun to sun

Walter's viburnum is one of the newest evergreen shrubs to become popular in landscaping. In the wild, it can grow up to 18 ft. tall and can be used as a screen or pruned into a hedge. The landscape selections are much smaller. The dainty clusters of early, small, white flowers produce clusters of small, dark, fleshy fruit that ripen in fall. It is important to insects and birds. Because it is not overly showy at any one time, and the fact that it is heat and drought tolerant, it may be best used as an evergreen shrub for its foliage affect, such as a substitute for dwarf yaupon holly. It is ideal in the deeper South and Florida, though the first cultivar has done well in Charlotte, North Carolina. Good 3 ft. cultivars are 'Mrs. Schiller's Delight', 'Reifler's Dwarf', and 'Whorled Class'.

Xanthorhiza simplicissima

yellowroot

shady streambanks

spring, summer, fall, winter

2–4 × 1–2 ft.

shade to part sun

This is a shrub with many features, including its ability to spread in average or moist to boggy soil and create a lush ground cover up to waist high in the shade. Be careful where you plant it as it may overtake less aggressive associates. The very early spring flowers are unusual, looking like emerging clusters of purplish stars. The autumn leaf colors are a stunning mix of red, yellow, and purple. Its bright yellow roots give this plant its common name, and are used as dye and herbal medicine. With their pointy green buds, the naked stems look like ornamental sticks and are interesting in winter. Yellowroot may become one of your favorite shrubs as it is ours; it was the first wild plant Larry transplanted as a young botany student in 1968 (and it's still growing).

Yucca filamentosa

yucca

dry woods, sandy roadsides, and waste areas

spring, summer, fall, winter

2–3 × 2–3 ft.

part sun to sun

Yuccas are striking (and sticking) plants. Their long leaves are sharp tipped and dangerous, so watch where you place them. These same leaves have intriguing, long white wisps of filamentous threads along the edges. In bloom, yucca is stunning with its branched inflorescences and large, creamy white flowers rising to 8 ft. above the leaves. Blooms are short lived, though. Yucca is especially quaint on coastal sand dunes. Many insects visit the night-fragrant flowers, including the ubiquitous small white moth that lives solely in the flowers, where it lays eggs after pollinating; the developing seeds feed the moth's young. This is a tough, clumping plant that seems both out of place and right at home in the Southeastern garden—depending on how you mix it in. Weakleaf yucca (*Yucca flaccida*) is similar, with smaller flowers and flexible, narrower leaves, but also with filamentous margins. It is native from Alabama and Tennessee, scattered east and west.

Zenobia pulverulenta

zenobia

coastal Carolinas, shrubby wetlands

spring, summer, fall, winter

2–6 × 2–3 ft.

part sun to sun

This can be a unique and beautiful plant, with charming masses of pendulous white flowers and whitish blue-green leaves. The fall foliage is fabulously multicolored, and some leaves are evergreen. It can also look a little disheveled if not grown in moist soil and good sun, and benefits from a little more cultural attention, such as trimming off old seed pods, especially if it is in a prime location. At its best, zenobia is a knockout in flower and leaf, especially when massed in a border. It can be semievergreen with shreddy winter bark. The ½ in. wide flowers are broadly cuplike, prompting the alternative common name of honey-cups. The cultivar 'Woodlander's Blue' is superb, with powder blue over purple fall foliage.

Trees

Sometimes homeowners will plant trees in anticipation of having a shade canopy in 10 or 20 years, but more often we plant small flowering trees for ornament. With that in mind, most of the selections presented in this chapter are of the latter nature. In the size information for each profile, we provide reasonable mature heights, which can vary depending on local conditions (though most can grow taller). We also list height only, not width—though generally, width is about two-thirds height. All trees recommended here are deciduous except as noted.

Additionally, we know that large home properties often retain remnants of forests that once grew there, and the tall trees that were part of those forests. Such trees can provide desirable shade or background, but homeowners also often have questions about which to remove if the need arises, and which to try to preserve. At the end of this chapter, we offer our thoughts on forest trees, and assessments of the most common species to be found in the Southeast.

Acer leucoderme

chalk maple

dryish Piedmont woods

spring, summer, fall

30 ft.

part sun to sun

Chalk maple is one of the finest small native trees we know of. Slow growing, with light-colored bark, it can reach 30 ft. tall. The best ones develop a crown that is rounded to upright. It is among the very last trees in autumn with color (usually peaking in early to mid-November) and is unrivaled in its brilliant dark reds and oranges. In many ways, chalk maple grows like a seed-grown (not grafted) Japanese maple—often with multiple trunks—and would be a suitable native substitute. It does fine in warmer climates, and is drought tolerant. This would be a good choice for a smaller garden or yard, but would take years to become a shade tree. The related larger forest tree for shade would be the slow-growing southern sugar maple, *Acer barbatum*, that can grow to 30–60 ft. over 30–40 years and has outstanding fall color. Do not plant northern sugar maple cultivars in warmer regions.

Acer pensylvanicum

striped maple

rich mountain forests

spring, summer, winter, fall

20 ft.

shade to part sun

Striped maple, or moosewood up North, is a small tree for all seasons. The big, lobed leaves are handsome, turning a wonderful autumn yellow; the flowers and fruit are interesting (but not particularly eye-catching); the winter twigs are noticeable; and the white-striped bark is outstanding. The tree struggles with the heat outside the mountains, but is worth trying in a woodland setting in the Upper South, with extra water during droughts.

striped maple leaves

striped maple bark

Acer rubrum

red maple

woods and swamps forests

spring, summer, fall, winter

60 ft.

part sun to sun

Red maple is a ubiquitous species in eastern North America, found in many habitats from wet to dry, and widely used as a street or home shade tree. Look for selections that come from your specific region and are known to do well in your climate. Do not plant a cheap, unnamed red maple! Otherwise, it is probably the best all-around choice for a fast-growing, colorful shade tree. One nice trait is that it blooms in late winter, with showy, bright red flowers and fruit, adding early color to the landscape. Two of the best cultivars for fall color in the Southeast are 'October Glory', which has a rounded crown, and 'Franksred' (better known as Red Sunset™), which is more upright. Do not plant silver maples (*Acer saccharinum*) as they are short lived and not heat tolerant in the Southeast.

red maple fruit (samaras)

▶ red maple leaves

Asimina triloba

pawpaw

low woods

spring, summer, fall, winter

25 ft.

shade to part sun

This fascinating small tree produces early spring flowers that are a joy to find—attractive, maroon, 1–2 in. wide, appearing along naked twigs as the leaves emerge in spring. The fruit is a large, greenish, aromatic, very fleshy and pulpy berry, 3–5 in. long, ripening in late summer to smell like tropical fruit and considered a prize find by wild food aficionados. Cultivars such as 'Potomac', 'Allegheny', and 'Shenandoah' have larger, more abundant fruit, the production of which is enhanced by planting in more sun (they love morning sun and moist soil) with another selection to cross pollinate. The rich yellow fall color is as good as any. Pawpaw forms colonies by root suckering, so either accept having a little grove in your back woods, or plant it in the lawn and mow around it. While it might not be as vigorous along the warm Gulf Coast, the species is found throughout the Southeast. All pawpaws are larval food plants for the lovely zebra swallowtail butterfly.

pawpaw leaves

◄ pawpaw flowers

Betula nigra

river birch

low woods and streambanks

spring, summer, fall, winter

60 ft.

part sun to sun

River birch is a tree widely used in home landscapes. Fast growing and sturdy, it is most attractive as a multitrunked specimen (with an odd numbers of trunks), showing its pendulous lower branches and attractive, salmon-colored, peely bark (its greatest asset). The early spring flowers are produced in attractive yellow male catkins. It does not tolerate drought and will begin to shed leaves in prolonged dry weather—shortening its life. It is perhaps the fastest growing shade tree and has minimal negative traits. Do not plant river birch too close to your house, as is often done, as they can become quite large in age. Keep it watered during droughts. River birch is the only heat tolerant birch—do not plant other birches.

Carpinus caroliniana

ironwood

streambanks and rich woods	
summer, fall, winter	
35 ft.	
shade to part sun	

The great attraction for ironwood is its fabulous bark that looks like smooth muscle, becoming more fluted with age. The wood itself is very hard. This tree does not like to be planted in full sun, especially in dry soil. It is a very informal tree and can have beautiful and distinctive character as an individual specimen, though it is never flashy in flower or leaf. Ironwood is often called musclewood, or simply hornbeam, which can be confusing, because many people feel the latter name is better reserved for eastern hop hornbeam (*Ostrya virginiana*). So be sure of what you are getting at the nursery or through mail order. Both species have similar leaves. Ironwood differs in having bark that is smooth rather than shreddy.

Cercis canadensis

eastern redbud

woods and disturbed roadsides

spring, summer, fall

25 ft.

part sun to sun

Redbud is one of our best known and most beautiful small trees. It is widely adaptable to various light and soil conditions, is drought tolerant, recovers from storm damage by sprouting from the base, and is a harbinger of spring with its cheerful pink flowers that are edible in salads. The tree is especially floriferous along the sunny edges of deciduous woods. It is our best fast-growing small tree for quick shade, effective after one or two full growing seasons under good conditions. There are many attractive cultivars involving flower and leaf color and plant form. 'Royal White' has pure white flowers; 'Appalachian Spring' is dark reddish purple; 'Traveller' is weeping; 'Hearts of Gold' and The Rising Sun™ are yellow-orange (fabulous); 'Forest Pansy' has purple leaves, but does not keep the color well in hot climates.

Chionanthus virginicus

fringe tree

dry woods

spring, summer, fall

20 ft.

part sun to sun

Seeing a fringe tree (also called grancy graybeard) in full bloom in a yard is a typical spring scene in the rural Southeast. This small tree (or big shrub) grows in dryish woods and in open areas. At its best, it is a multitrunked clump in mostly full sun, to about 15 ft. tall. Although a bit slow growing, it is worth the space for the white, fragrant, fleecy spring flowers and yellow fall colors. It can produce abundant purplish black, fleshy fruit in fall that birds love. Fringe tree seems so familiar, it will make you feel at home.

fringe tree flowers

Cladrastis kentukea*

yellowwood

rich mountain woods

spring, summer, fall, winter

50 ft.

part shade to sun

There is no finer tree for the landscape; yellowwood stands out in all seasons. It is a celebrated ornamental tree, with showy spring flowers that look like white wisteria clusters, excellent clean foliage, spectacular butter-yellow fall color, appealing smooth bark, and interesting branching structure. It may help to train (by selective pruning) young trees to ensure a desirable symmetrical growth pattern. Yellowwood does not bloom until it is about 10 years old, but it is worth the wait. Give it room in an open, sunny area and enjoy the scene. This is our favorite small tree.

*syn. C. lutea

Cornus alternifolia

pagoda dogwood

rich woods and streambanks

spring, summer, fall, winter

25 ft.

part shade to sun

This wonderful native dogwood has ornamental traits that have not been fully appreciated, and it should be more widely planted. It can be grown as a single- or multi-trunked tree or multitrunked shrub. It has excellent garden appeal in all seasons, not the least of which is the kaleidoscope of fall leaf colors that it can produce. The young twigs are smooth and shiny green, becoming reddish in winter sun; white stripes develop in the trunks as they mature. Leaves turn an intriguing array of red, orange, yellow, and purple in autumn. The small white spring flowers appear in flat-topped clusters 2–4 in. wide, on the tips of leafy branches which array themselves as tiers, or pagodas, along the trunk. The ¼ in. wide fleshy fruit are blue-black on red stalks, readily eaten by birds in late summer.

Cornus florida

flowering dogwood

deciduous woods

spring, summer, fall, winter

30 ft.

part shade to part sun

This species needs no introduction as it is the overall most beloved and widely planted deciduous tree of the Southeast. It has year-round appeal via flowers, foliage, form, fruit, and bark. It produces distinctive, layered branches forming a flat-topped crown with age, with bark that is thick and platy. Winter twigs are tipped with a single, large, onion-shaped flower bud. The true flowers are small, tight, hardly noticeable clusters surrounded by 4 large, showy, leaflike bracts, blooming in midspring. The early fall berries are relished by migrating birds and eaten quickly upon ripening. Wild flowering dogwood grows in shady woods, so planting it in full sun makes it look great, but is unhealthy for the tree and shortens its life. Many cultivars are available; 'Cloud 9' and 'Cherokee Princess' are two of the best for the Southeast, with big flowers. For a pink-flowering dogwood, select 'Cherokee Chief' or 'Cherokee Sunset'.

Cotinus obovatus

American smoketree

dryish woods

spring, summer, fall

30 ft.

part sun to sun

Smoketree, with its unique pinkish puffy plumes of tiny flowers and fruit in early summer, is delightfully unique in behavior. The 4 in. long, rounded, green waxy leaves make the tree look robust. It grows readily and rapidly in cultivation, creating a small tree with magnificent fall colors when grown in sun. 'Grace' is a choice hybrid, crossed with the commonly grown smoketree (*Cotinus coggygria*) of China.

Diospyros virginiana

persimmon

woods and disturbed places

spring, fall

50 ft.

part sun to sun

Possums love persimmon fruit—at least that what everybody thinks. You'll love it too, ripe, in puddings and pies (don't eat an unripe one.) But you won't love it if you plant a female next to your sidewalk. The fruit when it falls is messy, squishy, ooey, gooey, and all-around yucky! But the spectacular fall color—words cannot describe the intensity and richness—combined with the fabulous bark, will make you forgive and forget the fallen fruit mess. You may plant a persimmon tree (even a select one) for its tasty fruit, or you may already have one in a good location—away from walkways. The wood is one of the heaviest and hardest in North America. It may take two to cross pollinate for fruit.

persimmon fruit

persimmon bark

Franklinia alatamaha

Ben Franklin tree

river bluffs, extinct in the wild

spring, summer, fall, winter

12 ft.

part sun to sun

Franklinia alatamaha is one of our most celebrated species in the Southeast—right up there with flame azalea and Venus flytrap. It is certainly one of our showiest native woody plants. The large, 2–3 in. wide, white, late-summer flowers are followed by spectacular red-purple to orange-yellow fall color. The winter bark is interestingly striped. It is of historical importance because it disappeared from the wild in 1803 after discovery by John Bartram, but thrives in cultivation. Establishing can be tricky because it likes moist but well-drained soil. It is infamous for being easier to grow in a pot than in the ground. It did best for Larry when it was planted in very sandy soil and kept watered during droughts. There is a great semievergreen floriferous hybrid that is easier to grow and highly recommended—mountain gordlinia (× *Gordlinia grandiflora* 'Sweet Tea')—that captures most of the charm of pure Franklin tree. Water during droughts.

Halesia diptera

two-winged silverbell

bottomland forests

spring, fall

25 ft.

part sun to sun

Two-winged silverbell, from the Deep South, is a wonderful semiformal shrub or tree when grown in full sun, somewhat pyramidal and covered in spring with 1 in. wide white flowers. The deeply lobed, bell-shaped flowers are delightful, and with the plant's pleasing growth form and yellow fall color, it is an excellent choice for the Southeast. Silverbell has distinctive, striped bark. The large-flowered two-winged silverbell (*Halesia diptera* var. *magniflora*) has slightly larger flowers on a more informal, low-sweeping plant. Mountain silverbell (*H. tetraptera*) is considered one of the finest flowering trees, with true bell-shaped flowers in abundance, sometimes tinged with pink. It is a mountain forest tree to 70 ft., widely adaptable in the Upper South. While many people pronounce the Latin name "hal-*eeze*-ya" or "hal-*eese*-see-yah," you may choose to say "*hales*-ee-ah" to commemorate Stephen Hales, the man for whom it was named.

Ilex opaca

American holly

woods

spring, summer, fall, winter

50 ft.

part shade to sun

American holly is a beautiful and tough tree, surviving urban conditions. It is very cold hardy and our only broad-leaved evergreen forest tree that ranges northward. When grown in sun, a female specimen will become covered with the familiar red berries against spiny, dull green leaves, creating a cheerful sight in winter—the quintessential Christmas wreath material. It is then startling to see a flock of cedar waxwings literally defruit the tree in mid-March. A nearby male holly is required for cross-pollination to have good fruit set. It may be difficult to find a pure American holly at nurseries, as they do not transplant well, but there are so many in surrounding woods that you might have one. We really like the handsome evergreen selection 'Maryland Dwarf', which slowly grows wider than tall, up to 4 or 5 ft., to use as a specimen or foundation plant under windows.

Juniperus virginiana

eastern red cedar

old fields and woods

spring, summer, fall, winter

40 ft.

part sun to sun

This scale-leaved evergreen conifer is so common in many parts of the Southeast that it may be viewed as a roadside and pasture weed, but individual trees can be quite handsome, and they should be used more in landscaping, especially in full sun. The blue, fleshy cones, which can be quite attractive as a mass in winter, are relished by cedar waxwings and other migratory birds. Several cultivar forms are available for use in a variety of landscape situations. 'Burkii' is a columnar cultivar with blue foliage, useful in border sentinel plantings; 'Grey Owl' has gray-green foliage, grows 3 ft. tall by 6 ft. wide and is popular in groupings and foundation plantings. Other selections come in various shades of green, and can be tall and narrow, short and spreading, wide, or globose. There is a form and color for every need.

Liquidambar styraciflua

sweetgum

forests, old fields, and disturbed places

spring, summer, fall, winter

80 ft.

part sun to sun

Sweetgum is the tree everyone loves to hate—for the persistent, spiny, seemingly useless gum balls. There is no more ubiquitous tree; it appears in any disturbed area. However, on the positive side—there is no native tree with a finer fall mixed-color display, many birds eat the tiny seeds, the crushed foliage smells sweet, and the branches may have intriguing winged twigs. But the real reason we single out sweetgum is for the cultivar selections. We especially recommend a columnar one called 'Slender Silhouette'. It is quite narrow (3–4 ft. wide), tall (40+ ft.), and fits in a small site, producing the same good fall color, but fewer spiky gum balls. Another wide column–pyramidal form worth considering is Emerald Sentinel®. A fruitless cultivar, 'Rotundiloba', has proven to be disease-prone, but we have heard reports of good success, so check your local sources.

Magnolia grandiflora

southern magnolia

coastal moist forests

spring, summer, fall, winter

50 ft.

part sun to sun

Southern magnolia is an aristocrat—at its best in a majestic, dark evergreen pyramid form, offering its classic floral fragrance. It has come to symbolize the warmth and friendliness of the South. But be mindful: it can attain a width of more than 40 ft. The 1 ft. flowers last 2 days, emitting an overpoweringly sweet scent. The hard fruiting cones ripen in late summer, ejecting dangling, bright red ornamental seeds that birds pick off like candy. Because it is usually planted conspicuously near the house, a not-so-handsome specimen can be an eyesore forever, so plant a named selection, not just an inexpensive seedling. And be forewarned—these trees are messy, with their big leaves and cones. 'Alta' is a columnar cultivar, suitable for screening. 'Bracken's Brown Beauty' is a tough, well-formed choice, with slightly twisted, dull green foliage. 'D.D. Blanchard' is more pyramidal, probably the best in form, with broad, shiny green leaves that are copper-brown underneath. 'Little Gem' and 'Teddy Bear' are excellent dwarfs.

Magnolia macrophylla

bigleaf magnolia

moist bottomland forests

spring, summer, fall, winter

30 ft.

part shade to sun

Bigleaf magnolia is truly a striking plant; words fail to convey the feeling of awe you experience upon seeing one for the first time. The 30–40 in. long leaves (with basal earlobes) are unequaled in size, and the tree is probably not suitable for a small garden—but don't be afraid to try one anyway. The huge 1 ft. flowers are fragrant in late spring. The seed cones produce orange seeds, relished by birds. It is very easy to cultivate and when grown in light shade, it is a spreading, graceful tree that flowers quite well. When grown in full sun, the branches and leaves are held more vertically, giving a more compact appearance. The huge dried leaves make interesting decorations, and when they fall you can't rake them, you just gather them up.

bigleaf magnolia flower

Magnolia virginiana

sweet-bay magnolia

swamps and floodplains

spring, summer, fall, winter

30 ft.

part sun to sun

Sweet-bay magnolia makes a wonderful large, semievergreen shrub—and can become a small tree. It can be used as a specimen or foundation plant, as a screen, or grown in a large container. The 2 in. wide, white, late-spring flowers are quite fragrant. Bright red seeds appear in late summer, and the form is pyramidal but not as dense as that of an evergreen holly. Many cultivar selections are available. 'Moonglow' is cold hardy and keeps more leaves; 'Green Shadow' is more oval. Sweet-bay is better kept as a multi-trunked shrub than a tree that becomes so tall you can't see the flowers. Cut down the trunks and they will readily resprout.

Nyssa sylvatica

black gum

moist and dry woods

summer, fall, winter

50 ft.

part sun to sun

Black gum, or sour gum, is one of the best native trees for fall color, consistently producing outstanding displays of red to red-purple. It typically forms a straight main trunk with branches that are almost horizontal, well worth noticing in winter. The blocky bark is handsome as well. The tiny green flowers are unobtrusive in spring, but the dark blue fall fruit are great for wildlife. It is disease free and long lived, and is our single choice for best all-around tree. Homeowners who have it on their property should leave it to grow and remove smaller surrounding trees. The following cultivars are better than the species as unusual, smaller, ornamental garden specimen trees: 'Zydeco Twist' has contorted branches; 'Autumn Cascade' has weeping branches; 'Wildfire' is fabulous as a fast-growing, broad-spreading small tree with reddish new growth, but is not for the small garden.

Ostrya virginiana

eastern hop hornbeam

dryish woods

spring, summer, fall, winter

30 ft.

part shade to part sun

This small tree, which is one of our favorites, has bark that looks like a cat has scratched it, giving it a finely shredded appearance, with pieces of bark curled out and easily picked off. The bark is the tree's main ornamental feature, but the clusters of light-colored fruit look like dried hops and have some appeal. In some cities, it is used as a small, tough, street tree in hell strips. Unfortunately, the common names "ironwood" and "hornbeam" are often used interchangeably for *Ostrya* and *Carpinus* species. There is no confusing the plants, just their names, so take care when ordering by mail.

Oxydendrum arboreum

sourwood

moist to dry woods

spring, summer, fall, winter

40 ft.

part sun to sun

Found only in the eastern United States, sourwood, or sorrel tree, is a splendid tree for all seasons: outstanding in flower, form, foliage, fall color, and bark. The summer flowers look like clusters of lily-of-the-valley, and they are the source of sourwood honey in the mountains. Fall fruit are tan, dry clusters that look good with the spectacular pinkish red fall color, and persist into winter. The handsome bark is deeply blocky and ridged. To confirm its identity (the leaves can resemble black cherry and silverbell), just nibble a leaf (it has tiny teeth along the edges) to detect the sour taste. It is best grown in good sun to achieve characteristic form, abundant flowering, and wonderful fall color. The tree is a bit difficult to transplant and establish, but it's worth being persistent. Start with a small selection and don't let it dry out the first year.

Pinus glabra

spruce pine

moist hardwood forests and bluffs

spring, summer, fall, winter

30 ft.

part shade to part sun

We don't normally think of planting messy, sun-loving, ungainly pines as garden ornamentals, but this species is different—a neat, handsome, fine-textured tree for mostly shaded Southeast landscapes. It holds its spirally twisted, 3 in. long needles a long time on lower branches that may last for decades. The bark is tight like a spruce, not flaky like most pines. We think it's the most ornamental of the native pines. Sand pine (*Pinus clausa*) is similar, but the bark is flaky; to 40 ft. tall, and a windbreak or habitat cover in areas of infertile coastal sands. Beautiful white pine, *Pinus strobus*, of the mountains, has soft needles, is beautifully blue-green, and grows fast in shade to a large size. It is not heat tolerant, but try it in the Upper South, out of hot afternoon sun. There are several dwarf ('Nana') and weeping ('Pendula') cultivars that are much better than the species in the small garden.

Prunus caroliniana

Carolina cherry-laurel

thickets, low woods, coastal forests

spring, summer, fall, winter

25 ft.

part sun to sun

Carolina cherry-laurel is related to the more widely planted English cherry-laurel and could be a substitute. This is a good evergreen and is widely adaptable. It is one of the most common volunteer seedlings in shady thickets, where it is spread by birds. At its best, in good sun, it forms a handsome small tree with glossy evergreen foliage, delightful white spring flowers, and black hard berries (which could be a nuisance) for winter birds. Quite heat tolerant, it makes a wonderful screen in sun or light shade, and can be sheared into a hedge. Two nice cultivars are more refined: 'Bright 'N Tight' and 'Compacta'. It is salt-spray adaptable for beach property.

Prunus serotina

black cherry

forests, floodplains, disturbed areas

spring, summer, fall, winter

60 ft.

part sun to sun

Black cherry is a ubiquitous forest tree with attractive bark, shiny and peeling horizontally when young. With age, a flaky bark develops that we call potato chip bark. Maturing relatively early in its fast-growing life, it produces clusters of white spring flowers that bees like; these develop into juicy, dark-red "cherries" in summer that birds love—they can even become "drunk" eating the fermenting fruit. In fall, the color is gorgeous shades of red and yellow. It is also a host plant for many beautiful butterflies; for this reason, the tree is susceptible to disfigurement by tent caterpillars in spring. So: a tree that is especially useful to wildlife, but at the possible cost of unsightliness. Don't plant one, but don't get rid of it prematurely. Enjoy the flowers, fruit, and fall color. Monitor the tree's health, and as it fails, cut it to use the beautiful wood for furniture or great-smelling firewood.

Sabal palmetto

cabbage palmetto

coastal scrub communities

spring, summer, fall, winter

20 ft.

sun

Cabbage, or sabal, palmetto (the state tree of South Carolina) is the only native palm that makes a trunked tree outside of sub-tropical Florida. It is now being successfully planted far north of its range, where it can survive snow and single digit temperatures if water does not freeze in the crown. The blue-green, palm-pleated leaves grow in a shaggy crown; bees love the flowers and many animals like the abundant blackish berries. There are two secrets to successful transplantation (most die after transplanting). First, plant in pure sand, not too deep, in late spring. Then, most importantly, water it daily and well—into the top of the crown the first summer (at least), or during any period of very hot, dry weather. It may take two or more years to begin to form full-sized leaves after the first summer. It will eventually become stunning.

Sassafras albidum

sassafras

forests, fields, and roadsides

spring, summer, fall, winter

40 ft.

part sun to sun

Sassafras is a beloved tree; often the first one kids learn about when they are shown how the leaves are like mittens or gloves, depending on the number of lobes. The clusters of yellow flowers are the first of spring to open, and its leaves offer incomparable red-orange-yellow fall color. The tree starts out in old fields and grows up with the forest to persist as an isolated tree. If you cut down a large trunk, it will resprout readily from the roots, to form a colony. The attractive fruit are eaten by birds as soon as they turn red. Like other members of the laurel family, sassafras is the larval food of the peculiar tiger swallowtail caterpillar—the one with the big fake eye behind the head to fool (or scare) predators. Sassafras roots were once used to make root beer, and the very deep, blocky bark is gorgeous on large specimens.

Taxodium ascendens

pond cypress

coastal lake margins and swamps

spring, summer, fall, winter

50 ft.

part sun to sun

Pond cypress is one of our greatest southeastern ornamental species. We cannot say enough good things about its delicate beauty. It is closely related to the famous bald cypress (*Taxodium distichum*), but pond cypress does not become nearly as massive, makes smaller knees, and much better suited to smaller properties. It has deciduous, needlelike leafy branchlets that turn various shades of orange to reddish brown in autumn before falling to make a soft mat of litter, along with 1 in. round seed cones. It is fast growing and adaptable to wet or dry soils, in sun or part sun, but performs especially well in a pond margin or that permanently troublesome wet spot. The cultivars 'Prairie Sentinel' and 'Morris' (sold under the name Debonair™) are excellent selections.

Thuja occidentalis

eastern arborvitae

dryish woods

spring, summer, fall, winter

30 ft.

part shade to sun

Eastern arborvitae is a scale-leaved evergreen conifer, a standard among landscape plants. It is more of a northern species and may feel the stress of southern heat in the Deep South, so protect it there from afternoon sun. We like the toughness and rounded columnar profile of the 15–20 ft. cultivar 'DeGroot's Spire', which bronzes in full winter sun. Other heat-tolerant cultivars are 'Golden Globe', 2–3 ft.; 'Malonyana', rigidly upright like a pole, 15 ft.; 'Lutea', pyramidal to 30 ft.; 'Nigra', pyramidal to 20 ft. and green in winter. The best all-around selection is *Thuja occidentalis* 'Emerald Green', a very compact, narrow pyramid to 15 ft. that stays green and is good for screening and borders. Don't let it get too dry or too wet—we recommend watering new plants every week during droughts. Western arborvitae (*T. plicata*) cultivars such as 'Green Giant' and 'Zebrina' are better choices for full sun in the Upper Southeast.

Forest Trees

Many home properties in the Southeast are on wooded sites where a mature forest has been cleared to build the house and yard. The trees that remain are remnants of that forest, often up to 100 ft. tall. Typically, these trees are of good quality and well established after decades of growth, though construction activity can weaken some. Forest trees provide shade, a beautiful array of fall colors, a buffer from surrounding neighbors, and places for birds and wildlife to live. In fact, the caterpillars that feed on such trees are a main source of food for young birds. In short, your piece of forest should provide a pleasant background for your family activities. We have not written about the majority of forest trees individually in the previous profiles because average homeowners are not likely to plant them—they take too long to grow. We have focused on small flowering trees that work well as ornamentals, and we've included a few forest trees—such as sweet gum and black cherry—for specific reasons.

However, it's wise to consider the quality of forest trees. If you found yourself wanting to plant for the future, or you needed to remove trees for further construction, what choices would you make? The following considerations could help in your decisions.

From our standpoint, trees come in three categories: the best, the so-so, and the less-desirable.

The best trees are sturdy, long lived, generally disease free, and have attractive fall color. While you may not plant them, you should certainly keep them in your forest. These include, but are not limited to, basswood, beech, birch, black gum, hemlock (in the mountains mostly; be aware of the hemlock adelgid insect problem), hickory, magnolia, oak, red cedar, red maple, sassafras, sugar maple, and white ash (though these are soon to be attacked by the destructive emerald ash borer beetle that will kill white ash unless they are treated).

The so-so group includes those that you might have and might keep, but should not plant. They have fewer stellar traits than the first group, certainly may have some beauty (for example, sycamore's white bark), and are useful to wildlife, but could be removed without fear of losing a valuable specimen. These could be species with messy leaves and fruits, poor color, brittle trunks, or short lives. They include black cherry, black walnut, hackberry, many pines, Osage orange, pecan, sweetgum, sycamore, tulip poplar, and willow.

The third group is made up of species that generally have such detrimental traits (though they may have some value to wildlife) that they are undesirable to keep and certainly shouldn't be planted. These include black locust, boxelder maple, elms (susceptible to Dutch elm disease), green ash, honey locust, red mulberry, silver maple, and some pines (brittle limbs in ice storms). Some of these are short lived in nature.

These categories are, of course, based on a mixture of value judgments, and you may have reasons for wanting or not wanting a certain tree or species. There are beautiful specimens of the most troublesome trees. But be aware that some become liabilities as they age. To find out what to consider in your region, consult local experts. Sometimes (we like this philosophy) a tree is a tree and you may be inclined to tolerate something less than ideal because it is your only tree. Finally, look for the beauty in all of nature—because each member of the web of life has a seat at the table and brings something useful to the picnic.

Hardiness and Heat Zone Chart

USDA Plant Hardiness Zones

TEMP °F	ZONE	TEMP°C
−60 to −55	**1a**	−51 to −48
−55 to −50	**1b**	−48 to −46
−50 to −45	**2a**	−46 to −43
−45 to −40	**2b**	−43 to −40
−40 to −35	**3a**	−40 to −37
−35 to −30	**3b**	−37 to −34
−30 to −25	**4a**	−34 to −32
−25 to −20	**4b**	−32 to −29
−20 to −15	**5a**	−29 to −26
−15 to −10	**5b**	−26 to −23
−10 to −5	**6a**	−23 to −21
−5 to 0	**6b**	−21 to −18
0 to 5	**7a**	−18 to −15
5 to 10	**7b**	−15 to −12
10 to 15	**8a**	−12 to −9
15 to 20	**8b**	−9 to −7
20 to 25	**9a**	−7 to −4
25 to 30	**9b**	−4 to −1
30 to 35	**10a**	−1 to 2
35 to 40	**10b**	2 to 4
40 to 45	**11a**	4 to 7
45 to 50	**11b**	7 to 10
50 to 55	**12a**	10 to 13
55 to 60	**12b**	13 to 16
60 to 65	**13a**	16 to 18
65 to 70	**13b**	18 to 21

AHS Plant Heat Zones

ZONE	NUMBER OF DAYS PER YEAR ABOVE 86°F (30°C)
1	<1
2	1–7
3	>7–14
4	>14–30
5	>30–45
6	>45-60
7	>60–90
8	>90–120
9	>120–150
10	>150–180
11	>180–210
12	>210

Recommended Reading

Gardening

Armitage, Allan M. 2006. *Armitage's Native Plants for North American Gardens*. Portland, Oregon: Timber Press.

Burrell, C. Colston. 2006. *Native Alternatives to Invasive Plants*. Brooklyn, New York: Brooklyn Botanic Garden.

Cullina, William. 2000. *Guide to Growing and Propagating Wildflowers of the United States and Canada*. New York: Houghton Mifflin.

Darke, Rick, and Doug Tallamy. 2014. *The Living Landscape*. Portland, Oregon: Timber Press.

Dove, Tony, and Ginger Woolridge. 2018. *Essential Native Trees and Shrubs of the Eastern United States*. Watertown, Massachusetts: Bunker Hill Studio Books.

Holmes, Roger, and Rita Buchanan. 2010. *Southeast Home Landscaping*. Mawhah, New Jersey: Creative Homeowner.

Hunter, Margie. 2002. *Gardening with the Native Plants of Tennessee*. Knoxville, Tennessee: University of Tennessee Press.

Loewer, Peter. 2003. *Ornamental Grasses for the Southeast*. Nashville, Tennessee: Cool Springs Press.

Mellichamp, Larry, and Will Stuart. 2014. *Native Plants of the Southeast*. Portland, Oregon: Timber Press.

Moir-Messervy, Julie. 2009. *Home Outside: Creating the Landscape you Love*. Newton, Connecticut: Taunton Press.

Moore, Kathleen A., and Lucy Bradley. 2018. *North Carolina Extension Gardener Handbook*. Raleigh, North Carolina: North Carolina State Extension.

Nelson, Gil. 2010. *Best Native Plants for Southern Gardens: A Handbook for Gardeners, Homeowners and Professionals*. Gainesville, Florida: University Press of Florida.

Rainer, Thomas, and Claudia West. 2015. *Planting in a Post-Wild World*. Portland, Oregon: Timber Press.

Reeves, Walter, and Erica Glasener. 2007. *Month-by-Month Gardening in Georgia*. Nashville, Tennessee: Cool Springs Press.

Steffen, Richie, and Sue Olsen. 2015. *The Plant Lover's Guide to Ferns*. Portland, Oregon: Timber Press.

Steiner, Lynn M. 2016. *Grow Native: Bringing Natural Beauty to your Garden*. Nashville, Tennessee: Cool Springs Press.

Varlamoff, Susan M. 2016. *Sustainable Gardening for the Southeast*. Gainesville, Florida: University Press of Florida.

Wasowski, Sally. 2009. *Gardening with Native Plants of the South*. Dallas, Texas: Taylor Publishing.

Black, Scott Hoffman, et al. 2016. *Gardening for Butterflies*. Portland, Oregon: Timber Press.

Natural History

Barry, John M. 1980. *Natural Vegetation of South Carolina*. Columbia, South Carolina: University of South Carolina Press.

Finch, Bill. 2012. *Longleaf, Far as the Eye Can See: a New Version of North America's Richest Forest*. Chapel Hill, North Carolina: University of North Carolina Press.

Green, Charlotte Hilton. 1939. *Trees of the South*. Chapel Hill, North Carolina: University of North Carolina Press.

Jeffries, Stephanie B., and Thomas R. Wentworth. 2014. *Exploring Southern Appalachian Forests*. Chapel Hill, North Carolina: University of North Carolina Press.

Peattie, Donald C. 1939. *Flowering Earth*. New York: G.P. Putnam's Sons.

Stein, Sara. 1995. *Noah's Garden: Restoring the Ecology of Our Own Back Yards*. New York: Houghton Mifflin Harcourt.

Tallamy, Douglas W. 2007. *Bringing Nature Home*. Portland, Oregon: Timber Press.

Field Guides and Identification

Bell, C. Ritchie, and Anne H. Lindsey. 1990. *Fall Color and Woodland Harvests*. Chapel Hill, North Carolina: Laurel Hill Press.

Case, Frederick W., and Roberta B. Case. 1997. *Trilliums*. Portland, Oregon: Timber Press.

Cotterman, Laura, Daiman Waitt, and Alan Weakley. 2019. *Wildflowers of the Atlantic Southeast*. Portland, Oregon: Timber Press.

Horn, Dennis, and Tavia Cathcart. 2005. *Wildflowers of Tennessee, the Ohio Valley and the Southern Appalachians*. Auburn, Washington: Lone Pine Publishing.

Hosier, Paul E. 2018. *Seacoast Plants of the Carolinas: A New Guide for Plant Identifications and Use in the Coastal Landscape*. Chapel Hill, NC: University of North Carolina Press.

Kirkman, L. Katherine, Claud L. Brown, and Donald J. Leopold. 2007. *Native Trees of the Southeast*. Portland, Oregon: Timber Press.

Midgley, Jan. W. 1999. *Southeastern Wildflowers*. Birmingham, Alabama: Crane Hill Publishers. Note: there is a series of these for many individual states.

Porcher, Richard D., and Douglas A. Rayner. 2001. *A Guide to the Wildflowers of South Carolina*. Columbia, South Carolina: University of South Carolina Press.

Spira, Timothy P. 2011. *Wildflowers and Plant Communities of the Southern Appalachian Mountains and Piedmont*. Chapel Hill, North Carolina: The University of North Carolina Press.

Taylor, Walter K. 2013. *Florida Wildflowers: A Comprehensive Guide*. Gainesville, Florida: University Press of Florida.

Resources

Mail Order Nurseries

Almost Eden
Merryville, LA
Almostedenplants.com

Forest Farm
Williams, OR
Forestfarm.com

Gardens in the Wood of
Grassy Creek
Crumpler, NC
Gardensinthewood.com

Growing Wild
Siler City, NC
Growingwildnursery.com

Lazy K Nursery
Pine Mountain, GA
www.lazyknursery.com/wholesale_
nursery.html

Mail Order Natives
Lee, FL
Mailordernatives.com

Naturescapes of Beaufort, SC
Beaufort, SC
Naturescapesofbeaufort.com

Nearly Native Nursery
Fayetteville, GA
Nearlynativenursery.com

Nurseries Caroliniana
North Augusta, SC
Nurcar.com

Overhill Gardens
Vonoroe, TN
Overhillgardens.com

Pine Ridge Gardens
London, AR
Pineridgegardens.com

Plant More Natives
VA
Plantmorenatives.com

Plant Delights
Raleigh, NC
Plantdelights.com

Sunshine Farm and Gardens
Renick, WV
Sunfarm.com

Woodlanders, Inc.
Aiken, SC
Woodlanders.net

Wood Thrush Natives
Floyd, VA
Woodthrushnatives.com

Southeastern Public Gardens with Significant Native Plant Collections

Alabama
Birmingham Botanical Gardens
Donald E. Davis Arboretum at Auburn
University, Auburn AL
Huntsville Botanical Garden
Mobile Botanical Gardens (Longleaf
Pine Forest)
University of Alabama Arboretum,
Tuscaloosa, AL

Delaware
Mt. Cuba Center, Hockessin, DE

Florida (northern only)
Kanapaha Botanical Gardens,
Gainesville, FL

Georgia
Atlanta Botanical Garden
Atlanta History Center
Botanic Garden at Georgia Southern
University, Statesboro, GA
Georgia State University Perimeter
College Native Plant Botanical
Gardens, Decatur, GA
Lockerly Arboretum, Milledgeville, GA
State Botanical Gardens of Georgia,
Athens, GA

Mississippi
Crosby Arboretum, Picayune, MS

North Carolina
The Botanical Gardens at Asheville
Daniel Boone Native Gardens,
Boone, NC

Daniel Stowe Botanical Garden
(Piedmont Prairie), Belmont, NC
Highlands Botanical Garden at the
Highlands Biological Station,
Highlands, NC
Juniper Level Botanic Garden,
Raleigh, NC
North Carolina Arboretum,
Asheville, NC
North Carolina Botanical Garden,
Chapel Hill, NC
Sarah P. Duke Gardens, Durham, NC
Southern Highlands Reserve (by
appointment), Lake Toxaway, NC
UNC Charlotte Botanical Gardens,
Charlotte, NC

South Carolina
Brookgreen Gardens, Murrells
Inlet, SC
Kalmia Gardens (Black Creek
Floodplain), Hartsville, SC
Moore Farms Botanical Garden (by
appointment), Lake City, SC
State Botanical Garden of South
Carolina, Clemson, SC

Tennessee
Knoxville Botanical Garden and
Arboretum
Memphis Botanic Garden

Virginia
Green Spring Gardens,
Alexandria, VA
Hahn Horticulture Garden at
Virginia Tech, Blacksburg, VA
Lewis Ginter Botanical Garden,
Richmond, VA
Norfolk Botanical Garden
Orland E. White Arboretum at
Blandy Experimental Farm,
Boyce, VA

Washington, DC
United States Botanic Garden

Acknowledgments

This book was preceded by Larry and Will's book *Native Plants of the Southeast* (Timber Press, 2014) which was a true labor of love and culmination of lifetimes of learning, teaching, photographing, exploring, and being completely enthralled with the natural wonders of the Southeast. So many people both directly and indirectly contributed to that book, and our gratitude to them bears repeating. Paula would like to thank Larry and Will for inviting her to contribute to this book. It has been an honor. She would like to thank Richard Gross, Mary Griggs, Tammy Blume, Ed Davis, Meredith Hebden, Mae Lin Plummer, and Mariah Huffman for inspiration and for being there in a pinch. She would also like to thank her teachers, fellow graduate students, and finally, her own students for inspiring her to write about what she loves.

We would like to thank the following institutions for allowing us to take photographs: Southern Highlands Reserve, North Carolina Botanical Garden, Sarah P. Duke Gardens, University of North Carolina at Charlotte Botanical Gardens, Highlands Botanical Garden, South Carolina Botanical Garden, Elizabeth Lawrence House and Garden, Atlanta Botanical Garden, and Birmingham Botanical Gardens.

Special thanks go to Lisa Tompkins for sharing her expertise. Thanks also to the staff of the UNC Charlotte Botanical Gardens for always being there to bounce ideas off of and search for plants and photos. From the Highlands Botanical Garden, thanks to Bryding Adams, Margie Bauer, Chan Chandler, Lynda Anderson and Ken Conover, Helen and Russ Regnery, Liz Sargent, and Dollie Swanson. Thanks also to Beth Davis, Carol & Jon Fox, Tom Harville, Diane Laslie, Robert Jones, and Lynda and George Waldrep from the North Carolina Native Plant Society. Further thanks to David Campbell, Bob Oelberg, Amy Tipton, Janice Coffey Swab, Jean Hunnicutt, Don Fisher, Bob Gilbert, Karen Lawrence, and Stan Polanski.

Finally, we thank our families—near and extended—for their support, love, and encouragement. We couldn't be who we are and share it with others without you all.

Photography Credits

All photographs by the authors except as noted below.

Stephanie Brundage, courtesy of Lady Bird Johnson Wildflower Center, page 149
Connie Byrne, page 237
Alan Cressler, page 144 right
Jeff Reimer, courtesy of SelecTree, page 216 right
R.W. Smith, courtesy of Lady Bird Johnson Wildflower Center, page 116 right

Index

Dr. Larry Mellichamp, PhD, is professor emeritus of botany and horticulture at the University of North Carolina at Charlotte, where he taught for more than 39 years. He was also director of the University's Botanical Gardens, which has 10 acres of outdoor gardens, including the Mellichamp Natives Terrace Garden, which demonstrates the use of natives directly for the homeowner. Larry is an expert on native trees, shrubs, and wildflowers. He is also the recipient of the Tom Dodd, Jr. Award of Excellence from the Cullowhee Native Plant Conference.

Paula Gross holds a master's degree in horticulture from the University of Georgia, and currently teaches horticulture as an adjunct professor at Central Piedmont Community College in Charlotte, North Carolina. As the former associate director of the University of North Carolina at Charlotte Botanical Gardens, she co-led the growth of the gardens and greenhouses and led the creation of children's and adult programs, with the goal of building meaningful and diverse relationships between plants and people. She is co-author with Larry Mellichamp of *Bizarre Botanicals,* as well as a contributing writer for *Fine Gardening* magazine.

Will Stuart has been photographing wildflowers since the mid-1970s when he began supplementing his botany lectures with up-close portraits of the local flora of upstate New York. He is a certified native plant specialist, a member of the North Carolina Native Plant Society, the Audubon Society, the National Wildlife Federation, and the Carolina Nature Photographers Association. He is also is a contributing photographer to NameThatPlant.net and the Lady Bird Johnson Wildflower Center.